Published by
TÜRKİYE DİYANET VAKFI
YAYIN MATBAACILIK VE TİCARET İŞLETMESİ

Mithatpaşa Cad. 62/B 06420 Kızılay / ANKARA
Tel: 0.312 425 27 75 • 418 59 49
Faks: 417 00 09

ISBN 975-389-108-3
02.06.Y.0005.112

This book has
been recommended
by the resolution dated 24.04.1993 no: 13
of the Turkish Religious Foundation's Publication Board

PUBLICATIONS BY THE TURKISH RELIGIOUS FOUNDATION/112

THE BASICS OF ISLAM

(CREED, WORSHIP)

WITH AN ILLUSTRATED ABLUTION AND PRAYER GUIDE

Dr. Niyazi KAHVECİ

ANKARA / TURKEY
2002

•

Fourth Edition: June 2002, 1.000 ea.

CONTENTS

FOREWORD

My object in writing this brief and concise book has simply been to provide the average reader who has no access to the original sources, with a brief treatise giving a comprehensive and all-embracing the basic teachings of Islam i.e., Islamic belief and modes of worship Especially to the Muslims of the Western Hemisphere, particularly those young among them. This is a manual for English speaking muslims, and those who want to find out about the fundamentals of Islam. This book contains, rather detailed technical information on the duties of a muslim has to fulfil. Once the proper insight of Islam is obtained, the interested person can pursue the course of deeper knowledge on his own.

This manual, at the same time, aims a contribution to ease the worries of the parents who in a busy industrial society desparate and helpless in providing their children with religious guidance and instructions and teaching them the Islamic way of belief and worship. And of the parents who struggle to protect their children from being the victims of high pressure enviroment. It was prepared on the order of The Foundation of Turkish Religious Affairs in response to this urgent need.

In the book, simplicity of expression and clarity of ideas have been the main intent. For that purpose; the words of Arabic origin have been transliterated as they are pronounced, irrespective of transcriptional rules, e.g., salât instead of salâh, zakât instead of zakâh, in order to help the reader memorizing the Islamic terminology.

The book contains three chapters with several sections and units. The first chapter is about Islam; its meaning and its place among the Divine Religions. It describes the essential features of Islam. The second chapter articulates the articles of Islamic creed. The third chapter gives the outlook of the complete Islamic worships. Taking ablution and the performance of prayer have been illustrated so that those who wish to learn them without a teacher may have that opportunity.

In this modest work the references have been the publications of The Presidency of Turkish Religious Affairs which bears the endorsment of The Supreme Council For Religious Affairs of Turkey.

If this work is successful, it is by God's grace and guidance. But if it falls short of the readers expectations, we can only pray and hope that God will forgive our mistakes.

Dr. Niyazi KAHVECİ

SCHEME OF TRANSLITERATION

Consonents

ا ء	a	ز	z	ق	q
ب	b	س	s	ك	k
ت	t	ش	sh	ل	l
ث	th	ص	ş	م	m
ج	j	ض	d	ن	n
ح	h	ط	t	هـ	h
خ	kh	ظ	z	و	w
د	d	ع	'	ي	y
ذ	dh	غ	gh		
ر ـر	r	ف	f		

Short vowels		Long vowels	
ـَ	a	ـَا	a
ـُ	u		
ـِ	i	ـَى	a
		ـُو	u
		ـِي	ı

Diphtongs

ـَو	u
ـَي	i

Note:

ـة a, final, at, in construct form.

CHAPTER ONE
THE RELIGIONS AND ISLAM

SECTION ONE

WHAT IS RELIGION?

Religon is a set of divine principles which guide the wise-man to the happiness of two worlds.

There are three types of religion

1- True And Divine Religion *(al-Din al-Haq):*

It is the one sent to human being through a Messenger by Allah and have undergone no change and corruption. This only is the Religion of Islam.

2- Divine But Corrupted Religion *(al-Din al-Muharraf):*

It is the religion although it had originally been sent by Allah through a Messenger had undergone changes by the human being. Judaism and Christianity are of this kind.

3- Made-Up Religion *(al-Din al-Bâtıl):*

It is a made up religion by mankind and void at all times.

The Concept Of Religion

Throughout history there has allways been a religion. It may be divine or Man-made, for because it is a natural need. Some people used it as the means of exploitation and suppression, as a pretext for prejudice and persecution. Some other people used it as a source of power and domination over the masses. In the name of religion unjustifiable wars have been launched, freedom of thought and conscience has been oppressed, science has been persecuted, and man's dignity and honour have been debased. It, throughout history has been abused and misunderstood.

These are totally contrary to the Divine Religion's function, its concept and purpose. There are many religions in the world, and each one claims to be the one only true religion. Each religion is supposed to have come from God for the right guidance of man. But the results contradict their claims.

The Islamic concept of religion is unique. It is true that geniune religion must come from God for the right guidance of man. And it is equally true that human nature and major human needs are basically the same at all times. This conception leads to one conclusion, and that it is: There is only one true religion coming from the One and the same God, to deal with the outstanding human problems of all times. This religion is Islam. For because it complies with the conditions required in a Divine Religion, as the objectives and consequences.

SECTION TWO

ISLAM

What is Islam?

The word Islam derived from the Arabic root *'SLM'* which literally means, among other things, purity, peace, submission and obedience.

As a religion Islam means submission to the Will of God and obedience to His commands. It is through that submission that peace is brought about.

Islam Among Other Religions

The first man, Adam (a.s) at the same time is the first Messenger of God. The first Religion of mankind, therefore, it is a true one. Since then up to Jesus Christ, all the Prophets are to have had the mission of teaching the principles of God's Unity and worshipping Him. However these principles had been corrupted and their original versions disappeared. Allah had sent through Muhammed (s.a.w) to all mankind the perfect Religion of Islam thereof. Today, on the earth, the true Religion is only Islam. It is the only accepted Religion before Allah. As Allah has clearly put it: *"Surely, the Religion before Allah is Islam."* ('Ali Imran, 19).

The Message conveyed by the prophets before Muhammad was also Islam. The followers of Abraham and Moses as well as those of Jesus and the rest were all called Muslims. So Islam has been, and will continue to be, the true universal religion of God, because God is One and Changeless, and because human nature and major human needs are fundamentally the same, irrespective of time and place, of race and age, and of any other considerations.

The Objective Of Islam:

The objective of Islamic instructions is the providence of happiness to mankind, in this world and in the Next. Islamic Concept maintains that religion is not needed for only a spiritual and intellectual necessity and therefore it is for the next world as the concept of current Christianity is, and neither for only the needs of this world as the current Judaism beholds. It is for both. The Divine Religion should satisfy the spiritual and moderate material needs of man. It unites this world with the Next one to come. It educates the humanity to be respectful to human rights. Any religion fails to bear these fruits is not Islam or, is not religion at all. And any man who fails to draw these bnefits from religion is no religious.

The Instructions Of Islam Can Be Categorised As Such:

1- Belief.

2- Actions; This can be divided into two: Duties towards God ***('Ibâdât),*** and duties towards the creatures ***(Mu'âmalât)***

3- Ethics.

THE CHARACTERISTICS OF ISLAM

1- It is the last Religion

There will no religion be subsequent to Islam. Its instructions will last for ever. Muhammed is the last Prophet of Allah. No one will succeed him.

2- It is a universal Religion

The preceding religions had been confined to specific nations and only in a special region. Islam has been sent for all nations.

3- The instructions of Islam are well-sufficient to meet the requirements of all-mankind. Therefore no need arises for another religion.

4- Islam confirmes all preceding Divine-Religions, Prophets and Scriptures.

5- It abrogates all preceding Divine Religions, because they were sent for a limited period.

The Pecularities That Make Islam Universal

1- It is rational, logical and scientific Religion.

Islam has paid great attention to the wisdom and made it the primary condition for being eligible to religious duties. It equally pays importance to knowledge. It stresses on reading and learning, saying; it is obligatory to every male and female muslim.

2- It is a Religion for this world and the Next.

The dictum is "work for this world as if you will never die and work for the Next as if you are going to die tomorrow."

3- It is a Religion of easiness.

There is no hardship in Islam but easiness. As for the worships. For example in the prayer ***(salât)***. The traveller shortenes the obligatory ***(fard)*** prayers into two rek'ats. Who are unable to perform the prayer at standing up, fulfils them while sitting, or laying on a bed. The sick may not fast in the Ramadan month and substitute in another time. The ones who have incurable disease may never fast and pay ransom ***(fidya)*** instead, and so forth.

4- There is no exessiveness in Islam.

It is in conformity with the human-nature. The Islamic injuctions are the most appropriate to human-nature. Obedience to them is the muslims duty. It is a torture to the body to fulfil what is not a command of Islam as going exessive. Keeping himself away from the abundance which is lawful ***(halal).*** Living in a squallor while otherwise is possible has nothing to do with Islam.

5- Islam is a Religion of peace and love.

It enjoins the love of mankind and respect to human rights. Thus, it aims to provide an ever-lasting peace, social order and happiness.

Thereof Islam has laid certain principles and considered them as fundamental prequisites to be a true-believer.

Three Conditions Necessitate the Advent of Islam:

1- The earlier Divine-Religions have been distorted or corrupted or they have died and their revival is needed.

2- The earlier Divine-Religions were incomplete and it is necessary to amend them, improve on them or add something to them.

3- The earlier Divine-Religions were raised for a particular nation or territory, and a universal one is required.

By Islam God has completed His revealed guidance and made it a complete religion for all mankind. God has said that: *"Today I have perfected your religion for you, and have completed My bounty upon you."*

Islam is based on human nature which has remained the same in all times and epoch. All men are cast in the moulds of the earliest men and fundamental human nature remains unchanged.

CHAPTER TWO
THE CREED OF ISLAM

SECTION ONE

THE IDEOLOGICAL FOUNDATIONS OF ISLAM

How To become a Muslim?

To become a Muslim does not require a religious procession under the conduct of a clergyman nor it should be in a mosque.

To become a Muslim, even on ones own, pronouncing the 'Kalima Tawhid' or the 'Kalima Shahada' will be sufficient. This is a general belief ***(îmân ijmâlî)*** which is embodied in the kalima tawhid and in kalima shahada.

I- THE FORMULA OF GOD'S UNITY *(AL-KALIMA AL-TAWHID)*

لَآ اِلٰهَ اِلَّا اللّٰهُ مُحَمَّدٌ رَسُولُ اللّٰهِ

Transliteration:

La ilaha illallah Muhammad Rasûlullah.

Translation:

There is no deity but Allah. Muhammad is the Prophet of Allah.

The Religion of Islam is summed up as a principle in this sentence.

This is the expression which distinguishes a Muslim from a ***kâfir*** (unbeliever), a ***mushrik*** (polytheist) or a ***dahriya*** *atheist)*.

II- THE WORD OF TESTIMONY *(al-kalima al-shahâda)*

اَشْهَدُ اَنْ لَآ اِلٰهَ اِلَّا اللّٰهُ. وَاَشْهَدُ اَنَّ مُحَمَّدًا عَبْدُهُ وَرَسُولُهُ

Transliteretation:

Ashhadu an-lâ ilâha illallâh wa ashhadu anna Muhammadan 'abduhu wa Rasûluh.

Translation:

I bear witness that there is no deity but Allah and Muhammad is His servant and His apostle.

Iman should be held fast in mind *('aqd bi'l qalb),* testifying with the tongue *(shahâda bi'l lisân)* if necessary.

SECTION TWO

THE ISLAMIC FAITH *(ÎMÂN)*

The Prophet Muhammad (peace be upon him) articulated the Islamic faith *(îmân)* in this sentence; which is titled as *"Amantu"*. This is entitled as the detailed belief *(îmân tafsîlî)*.

آمَنْتُ بِاللّٰهِ وَمَلٰئِكَتِهِ وَكُتُبِهِ وَرُسُلِهِ وَالْيَوْمِ الْاٰخِرِ
وَبِالْقَدَرِ خَيْرِهِ وَشَرِّهِ مِنَ اللّٰهِ تَعَالٰى وَالْبَعْثُ
بَعْدَ الْمَوْتِ حَقٌّ
اَشْهَدُ اَنْ لَا اِلٰهَ اِلَّا اللّٰهُ وَاَشْهَدُ اَنَّ مُحَمَّدًا عَبْدُهُ وَرَسُولُهُ

Transliteration:

Amantu billâh wa malâikatihî wa kutubihî wa rusulihî wal yawmil âhiri wa bil qadari khayrihî wa sharrihi min allahi te'âla wal ba'thu ba'dal mawti. Ashhadu an-la ilâha illallâh wa ashhadu anna Muhammadan 'abduhu wa Rasûluh.

Translation:

I believe in God, in His angels, in His books, in His Prophets, in the day of judgement, in that good and evil fate comes from God, in resurrection after death. I bear witness that there is no deity but Allah and Muhammad is His servant and His apostle.

The Articles Of Faith

1- Belief in God

2- Belief in God's Angels

3- Belief in the Books of God

4- Belief in God's Prophets

5- Belief in Life after Death

6- Belief in Fate *(qadar);* the good and the evil are created by Allah.

Disbelief in any one of these articles lead to unbelief *(kufr).* Where there is no iman there is no Islam. Belief is the idological base of Islam.

The Categories of Mankind from the Belief Point of View

1- Believer *(mu'min):* He who believes in Allah and His oneness and that Muhammad is His apostle. The belief should be by heart and expressed verbally.

2- Hypocrat *(munâfiq):* Although has no belief at heart he manifests it orally:

3- Unbeliever *(kâfir):* He who does not believe in God and His apostle.

The Conditions for a Valid Belief

1- The belief should not be attested, for the first time, in the state of desperation. On the verge of death everybody will witness the Next world. The believing at this moment is not valid if there was not before.

2- Muslims should refrain from the actions and words denoting unbelief. For example; a person believing in all religious commands but denying the prayer. He loses his faith. This causes him unbelief. Since the items of religious belief must be in complete. Denial one of them is like rejecting all.

3- The muslim must believe that all the Islamic injunctions are perfect. Dislike any of them results to unbelief.

First of all one should have an unshakable belief in these articles. If one does not have that belief, he may fall prey to false gods, and consequently to invented beliefs.

SECTION THREE

FAITH IN GOD

Islam means obedience to God. Therefore belief in God is the first and main article of the Islamic faith. This obedience cannot be complete unless man knows certain basic facts pertinent to God.

First of all, one should have an unshakable belief in the existence and oneness of God. Without this obedience to Him being a believer is clearly impossible. Man has to believe in that because everything in the world proves that He exists. Belief in God and His great power alone can provide mankind with the best possible explanation of many mysterious things in life.

The Existence and Oneness of God

Every mature and wise person is obliged to believe in the existence of God and His oneness. He is the Creator of everything on earth and in the heavens. He is the Ruler and the Sustainer of the Universe and there is no one else to share the creativity with Him. He is Who has given the universe a complete code of life, and He is Who will annihilate them.

God can only be percieved by mankind through His Qualities and Attributions. A Muslim is obliged to know God as the Islamic concept describes Him.

The Attributions of Allah

Allah has fourteen attributions. Six of them are ***'Zâtî'*** and eight of them are ***'Subûtî'***.

Zâtî attributions

1- ***Vucûd*** (Existing)

2- ***Kıdem*** (Eternity)

3- ***Bekâ*** (Continuance)

4- ***Vahdâniyyat*** (Oneness)

5- ***Muhâlafat lil-havâdis*** (Difference from originated things)

6- ***Kıyam bi-Nafsih*** (Self-subsistence)

***Subûtî* Attributions**

1- ***Hayât*** (Living) Allah always is alive.

2- ***'Ilim*** (Knowledge): Allah Knows the past, the future, the known, the unknown and what passes through the intellects.

3- ***Semî'*** (Hearing): Allah hears everything.

4- ***Basar*** (Seeing): Allah sees the visible and invisible.

5- ***Irâda*** (Willing): Allah decreeses and implements.

6- ***Qudrat*** (All-Sustaining Power): Allah has an endless power.

7) ***Kalâm*** (Speech): Allah has words and passed some of them to His Messengers.

8- ***Takwîn*** (Bringing into being): Allah created everything. When decreeses, He says: "beget" and it begets. And destroyes whatever He wishses.

This is the Islamic way of acquiring the knowledge of God, and the description of Him explained by Himself through His Messenger Muhammad. Although with his wisdom, reason , and knowledge man might perceive God by the observation to the countless manifestation of Him surrounded him internally and externally. But man's intellect and capacity for knowledge is no immune from errancy. God, therefore, spared His human creatures such a hard test. Through His Grace and Benevolence He raised for mankind some men among themselves to whom He imparted the true knowledge of His attributions.

God forgives not that partners should be set up with Him. He forgives anything else, to whom He pleases. His love for the creatures is immense and beyond human imagination. We cannot measure or count His favors. He creates us and takes care of us. He never forgets us or lets down or ignores our sincere calls upon Him.

In return for all these great favors and kindness God does not need anything from us, because He is the Needless.

The Qur'an (39:53-54) says:

"Say: O my servants who have transgressed against their souls! Despair not of the Mercy of God: for God forgives all sins, for He is Most forgiving, Most Merciful. Turn to your Lord (in repentance) and submit to Him, before the penalty comes on you; after that you shall not be helped. And follow the best of the courses revealed to you from your Lord, before the penalty comes on you, suddenly while you perceive not."

SECTION FOUR

BELIEF IN GOD'S ANGELS

The second precondition for being a mu'min is to believe in the angels of God.

The Nature And The Features Of Angels

They have been created from light *(nûr)*. That is, they are the creatures of light.

They have no material body.

They are spiritual beings.

They have no physical desires nor material needs.

They do not eat, drink, sleep or get tired.

There is no masculinity or femininity for them.

They are the beloved servants of Allah. They do according to His commands. They do not desdain from His service, neither they are wearied. They have no share in God's divinity. They have no authority to do anything on their own accord. To worship them and to solicit their help is degrading and debasing for man. God had made them on the first day of man's creation, prostrate themselves before Adam, granted to him greater knowledge than they possessed and bestowed on Adam His own vicegerency on this earth in preference to them.

Allah has creatures in several shapes. Some of them are perceptible to human-eyes and some of them not. We cannot deny their existence just because we do not see them with our naked eyes, smell, or touch or taste or hear; yet we do acknowledge their existence. The human-eye is unable to see everything; such as, wisdom, weather, wind, gas and the electricity. But we know that they exist.

We are obliged to believe in the existence of the angels as

has been reported by the Qur'an and the Hadis (Tradition of the Prophet). The Prophet (s.a.w) saw the angels. They are not described as being male or female.

The statement of the idolators that the angels are the daughters of Allah is unacceptable, unsounded and extravagant. Just as the statement of the jews that one of the angels may commit sin of unbelief and be punished by Allah. Metamorphosis is also an extravagant statement.

The Angels And Their Duties

The angels are existant in heavens, on earth and everywhere. Their total number can only be known by Allah.

God Almighty entailed on the angels separate functions and manifests His power and omnipotence through them.

Some of the angels are responsible for taking the lives of those whose predestined moment of death arrives. While others charged with safeguarding the humanbeings are always present by their sides. Some others keep a record of good and bad deeds of mankind. The angels provide strength to the believers, intercede and invoke to God on behalf of human beings. Another group of angels is responsible for the arrangement of the universe and maintaining the order.

The Archangels and Their Duties

1-*Jabrâîl* (Gabriel)

His duty is acting as a mediator by carrying the message and the Scriptures from Allah to the Prophets.

2- *Mikâîl* (Michael)

He administers the affairs in the universe and in the nature. Such as bringing precipitation, controlling the air, wind to blow, and plants to grow.

3- *Isrâfîl* (Seraph)

His duty is to end the universe and to resurrect the humanbeing.

4- *Azrâîl* (Azrael)

He takes the lives of whose predestined time comes.

5- *Munkar* and *Nakîr*

The two angels who examine the dead in the grave as to his faith.

6- *Rıdvân*

The archangel of the Paradise.

7- *Mâlik*

The archangel of the Hell.

8- *Kirâman Katibîn*

They are the honorable recorders. They record every actions of mankind.

SECTION FIVE

FAITH IN THE BOOKS OF GOD

The third article of faith is to believe in the Books of God; books which He has sent down to mankind through His Prophets by the mean of revelation *(wahy).*

The Nature of Revelation *(Wahy)*

Wahy literally means inspiration and revelation.

Terminologically: What Allah reveals to His prophets. It is a certain information *('ilm yaqîn)*

The Forms of Revelation

1- Proper dream vision ***(ru'yâ sâdıqa):*** Allah may reveal some information He wished to His Prophets through dreams. The firs revelation to our Prophet was of this kind. What he saw in his dream had occured properly.

2- Inspiration ***(Ilhâm):*** Allah may inspire to His Prophets' hearts directly.

3- Auditon: Without a mediator and vision the Prophets hear Allah's speech.

4- Through an envoy: Allah may employ an angel, usually Gabriel, to convey His message to His Messengers.

THE DIVINE BOOKS AND PAGES

Allah has books which He has sent down to His Prophets. In them He has shown His positive commands and the prohibitions, His promise ***(wa'd)*** and His thread ***(wa'îd)*** in order to provide happiness of two world for mankind. All the divine books are the Speech of Allah. They were sent down in the same way as He sent down the Qur'an. We have been informed the names of some of these books.

The Main Books

1- ***Tawrât*** (Tora or Old Testament) to Moses (Musa)

2- ***Zabûr*** (Psalms) to David

3- ***Injîl*** (Gospel, New Testament) to Jesus Christ ('Îsâ)

4- ***Qur'ân*** to Muhammad

We have not been informed the names of the Books given to other Prophets. Therefore with regard to other Divine Books may exist, we are not in a position to say with certainty whether they were originally revealed books or not. But we also believe that some pages ***(subûf)*** sent down to the Prophets.

The Pages And the Prophets

1- 10 pages to Adem (Adam)

2- 50 pages to Şît (Sheet)

3- 10 pages to Idris (Enoch)

4- 10 pages to Ibrahim (Abraham).

These pages are extinct today. They are not traceable in existing world literature.

David's Zabûr, the Tora and the Injil exist with the Jews and the Christians. But the Qur'an informes us that these people have changed and added to these Books. God's words have been mixed up with the texts of their own making. These books are called corrupted ***(mubarraf).*** The Jews and the Christians admit that they do not possess their original texts and have only their translations which have been altered over many centuries and are being still changed.

The Muslims have been commanded to believe in previously revealed Books only in the sense of admitting that, before the Qur'an. God has also sent down Books through His Prophets. Therefore it is comprehensible that the sending of The Qur'an as a divine Book is not anew and strange event, but only confirmed, restated and completed those divine in structions which people had mutilated or lost in antiquity.

The fact is that the original Word of God is preserved neither with the Jews nor with the Christians. The Qur'an on the other hand is fully preserved and not a syllable has been changed or left out of it. It exists exactly as it was revealed to the Prophet. Allah has guaranteed its security and full protection. He says in the Qur'an: *"We sent it down and We will protect it."* Qur'an, Hicr, 9.

The former Divine Books were sent down in languages which died long ago. No nation or community now speaks those languages. The language of the Qur'an, on the other hand, is a living language. Each one of the existing Sacred Books has been addressed to a particular people in a restricted area. Each one contains a number of commands which seem to have been meant for a particular period of history, and which met the needs of that age only. They are not for the world. In contrast to this, the Qur'an is addressed to all mankind. Not a single injunction of it can be suspected as having been addressed to a particular people. In the same manner, all the commands and injunctions in the Qur'an can be acted upon at any place and in any age. That is to say, the Qur'an is meant for the whole world and is an eternal code for human life.

It is a fact that previous Divine Books also enshrined good and virtue. They also taught the principles of morality and truthfulness and presented the mode of living which was to God's pleasure. But none of them was comprehensive enough to embrace all that is necessary for a virtuous human life. It is the Qur'an only, which enshrined not only all that was good in the former Books but also perfects the way of Allah and presents it in its entirety and outlines that code of life which comprehends all that is necessary for man on this earth.

SECTION SIX

THE QUR'AN

The Qur'an is unique and eternal miracle of the Prophet Muhammad.

All the people of the world have been kept responsible to have faith in it.

It will be in effect until the Last Day. And there will be no other Divine Book succeeding It.

A Brief History of the Compilation of the Qur'an

The Revelation of the Qur'an

The first revelation of the Qur'an began in the 41st year after the birth of the Prophet. Its first Sura; al-'Alaq or al-Iqra was revealed in the Cave of Hira, where its first five verses were revealed on the 9th of Rabi'ul Awwal of the first year of the Prophethood (i.e. 12th February 610 A.D.).

The first verse starts with "Read" command. Here are the translation of the first five verses:

1- Read in the name of your Lord who created.

2- He created man from a clot.

3- Read, and your Lord is Most Honourable

4- Who taught with the pen.

5- Tauht man what he knew not.

The archangel Gabriel, on Allah's command directed to the Prophet Muhammad. Said to him: *"Read"*. He said: *"What shall I read?"* This had been repeated three times. Gabriel denounced the first five verses. And the revelation of the Qur'an has started.

In the early days Halid b. Sa'id accepted the Islam and the Holy Prophet asked him to scribe the portion of the revealed holy Book. In time, as many as fourty two scribes were appointed by the Prophet. Hanzala b. Rabi' was appointed as the Chief of the scribes whose duty was to remain with the Prophet all the time so that the scribing work may not be held in abeyance.

One of the scribes Zayd b. Sabit said:

"When a verse was revealed, the Prophet called me. I presented myself at once with the plate, pen and ink-pot. The Prophet used to dictate the revealed verses, asked me to reherse the Sura and get it corrected then it was ordered to be promulgated."

Under Divine Guidance the Holy Book was compiled, under different chapters, arrangement of verses etc. The entire Book was rendered into writing as it is today.

In the battle against the imposter (false prophet) Musaylama, many of the Muslims who were *hafiz* (who memorized the Qur'an) were martyred. This aroused in 'Umar (the second Caliph) the fear that some knowledge of the revelation might be difficult to find later on. So 'Umar induced the then Caliph Abû Bakr Sıddıq to begin the collection of the scattered discourse. The work was entrusted to the famous companion Zayd b. Sabit. He collected and presented the Qur'an to Abu Bakr, the then Caliph.

On the demise of Abu Bakr the Book passed into the hands of his successor 'Umar, who in turn bequethed it to his daughter Hafsa, the widow of the Prophet Muhammad. It was this same copy (Zayd b. Sabit's version) that formed the basis of the copies distributed on a large scale by the third Caliph 'Usman b. 'Affan.

DUTIES TOWARDS QUR'AN

1- Reciting the Qur'an in a proper and correct spelling in accordance with *tajwîd science.*

2- Handling It with *wudû* (ablution) and opening the recitation briefly with the *"A'ûdhu Basmala"*.

3- Showing respect to It since recitation of It, in away meant as if speaking to God.

4- Reciting It in the clean places.

5- Listening to Qur'an when It is recited.

6- The Qur'an must be placed in high places.

SECTION SEVEN

BELIEF IN GOD'S PROPHETS

The Need For A Prophet

The sending of Messengers means the sending of a creature between Allah and intelligent beings in order thereby to correct the defects by which their reasons have fallen short of the benefits of this world and the next.

The sending of a Messenger is necessary, not meaning it is incumbent to Allah, but meaning that wisdom *(hikma)* demands it, since in it there are wise and beneficial things. Allah has sent messengers of mankind to mankind announcing good tidings of the Garden *(Cennet)* and reward to the people of Belief and obedience. Warning the people of Unbelief and disobedience of the Fire *(Cehennem)* and punishment. For these are among the things of which Reason has no way of obtaining knowledge. And also Reason may be able to find God but fails to reconize His attributions and how to worship. Therefore it was of the grace of Allah and His mercy to mankind that He sent Messengers. They show the right path and the true ethics. They are mediators between God and His creatures.

Prophethood is the gift of God. He bestowes it upon whom He wishes and it cannot be obtained through a strife.

The Qualities Of the Prophets

The qualities necessary in a true Prophet are:

1- ***Sıdq*** (Veracity)

2- ***Amânat*** (Trustworthiness)

3- ***Fatânat*** (Intelligence)

4- ***'Ismat*** (Preserved from falsehood)

5- *Tablîgh* (Conveying the Message)

God has raised messengers among every people, and that thay all brought the same religion Islam, which the Prophet Muhammad propagated. In this respect all the Messengers of God stand on a par with each other. If a man believes any one of them, he as it were, believes all, and if a man affirms and believes in one of them, he must and ought to affirm all. Tradition has it that the total number of Prophets sent to different peoples at different times is 124000. We have to positively believe in those of the Prophets whose names have been mentioned in the Qur'an. Regarding the rest. Thus we believe in all the Prophets raised in India, China, Persia, Egypt, Africa, Europe and other countries of the world, but we are not in a position to be definite about a particular person outside the list of Prophets named in the Qur'an.

The Prophets Whose Names Mentioned In The Qur'an.

God Almighty informed us about some Prophets in the Qur'an. Their number is twentyfive.

The Holy Qur'an has mentioned the following names of the Prophets:

Adem (adam), Idris (Enoch), Nuh (Noah), Hud, Salih, Ibrahim (Abraham), Lut (Lot), Ismail (Ishmael), Ishak (Isaac) Yaqub (Jacob), Yusuf (Joseph), Shu'ayb, Harun (Aren), Musa (Moses), Davud (David), Suleyman (Solomon), Eyyub (Job), Zulkifl (John the Baptist), Yunus (Jonah), Ilyas (Elias), Elyesa (Elisha), Zekeriya (Zachariah), Yahya (Ezekiel), Isa (jesus) and Muhammad.

In Islam it is necessary to have implicit faith in all the Prophets of God. One who does not believe in a particular Prophet would be a *kâfir,* though he may be professing faith in all other Prophets.

The Commons Of The Messages Brought By The Prophets

All the Prophets of God have been deputed by Him to teach the same straight path of Islam. In this sense all Divine Religions share three common grounds.

1- The principles of Faith

2- Worships

3- Ethics

The guidance imparted through the Prophets of the past was not complete. Every Prophet was followed by another who affected alterations and additions in the teaching and injuctions of his predecessors. In this way the chain of reform and progress continued. That is why the teaching of the earlier Prophets, after the lapse of time were lost in oblivion. Obviously there was no need to preserve earlier teachings when amended and improved guidance had taken their place.

He who follows Muhammad followed all the Prophets. For whatever was good and eternally workable in their teachings has been embodied in his teaching. He is the last Prophet of God. After him no Prophet will appear among any people till the Day of Judgement.

Our Prophet's Biography

Born in 570 A.D. in Mecca

Mother's name: Amina

Father's name: 'Abdullah

He became Prophet of God in 610 A.D. at the age of 40

Emigrated to Madina: in 622 A.D.

Died in 632 in Madina

The Finality of Prophethood *(Khataman Nabiyyîn)*

The Qur'an says: *"Muhammad is the Messenger of God and*

the last of the Prophets" (Quar'an, 33; 40) The real death of a Prophet consists not in his physical demise but in the ending of the influence of his teachings. The earlier prophets have died because their followers have adultarated their teachings, distorted their instructions, and sullied their life-examples by attaching fictitious events to them. The life-histories of the earlier Prophets have been so mixed up with fiction that an accurate and auhentic account of their lives has become impossible. Their lives have become tales and legends and no trustworthy record is available anywhere. Thus, the real death of a Prophet consists in the death of his teachings.

None of these conditions exists for our Prophet. The account of his life and teachings is preserved with complete accuracy. It is as though it all happened yesterday rather than thirteen centuries ago. That is why after him there remains no need for new prophethood. Therefore he has been described by the Qur'an as *Khataman Nabiyyîn* (the last of the chain of the true Prophets).

SECTION EIGHT

BELIEF IN LIFE AFTER DEATH

The fifth article of Islamic Faith is belief in life after death. We are obliged to believe in resurrection and in the Day of Judgement.

The life of this world and of all that is in it will come to an end on an appointed date. Everything will be annihilated. That day is called ***Oiyâmat***., i.e., the Last Day.

All the humanbeings who have lived in the world since its inception will then be restored to life and will be presented before God. This is called ***Hashr*** (Resurrection).

The entire record of every person will be presented before God for final judgement ***(Hisâb).***

The one who excels in goodness will be rewarded. One whose evils and wrong doings outweight his good deeds will be punished.

Those who emerge successful in this judgement will go Paradise ***(Cannat)***. The doors of eternal bliss will be opened to them. Those who are condemned and deserved punishment will be sent to Hell ***(Cabannam)***. That Day Absolute Judgement will be done to all. That day the goodness will be rewarded and the evil will be arrested which the case might have been the contrary in the world by escaping from the mundane law and left out unrewarded and unpunished.

The Need And Effect Of This Belief

Belief in Life after Death has always been an essential condition for being a believer in every Religion. Every Prophet asked his followers to believe in it, in the same way as the last of the Prophets; Muhammad has asked us to do. All Prophets have categorically declared that one who does not believe in it, casts doubts on it, is a *kafir*. This so because denial of it makes all other beliefs meaningless. This denial destroyes the very sanction for a good life.

In the very nature of man, he instinctively regards a useless action as totally unnecessary. Now think of the man who believes in the Day of Judgement. It's acceptance determines the very course of his life and behaviours. He will look on things in their wider perspective and always keep the permanent benefit or harm in view. He will do the good, however costly it may be to him in terms of worldly gains, or however injurious it may be to his immediate interests. He will avoid the wrong however tempting it may look. He gives no boder to their worldly gains and interests. He will not put his eternal bliss at stake for a passing gain. He will definitely become a constracting member of his society. He will be confident that God will reward him for the losses and will punish him for unjust gains, however he might escape punishment in his short worldly life. Another benefit of this belief is providing solace for the losses.

SECTION NINE

BELIEF IN FATE *(QADAR)*

Qadar means that God has the eternal knowledge of minute details of all things that will happen, before they actually take place.

God gives man the right of selection and self determination. He is free to do as he wishes. Therefore he is held responsible for his actions. Man desires, decides and plans but God creates his deeds. This is what is meant by 'good or evil takes place with God's consent.'

Belief in *qadar* does not in any way make man fatalist or helpless. It simply draws the demarcation line between what is God's concern and what is man's responsibility. The timeless knowledge and power of God to execute His plans do not prevent us from making our own plans in our own limited sphere of power. If we fail we should tray again and again, or at least, try to increase our power first if necessary. What is beyond our capacity we are not held responsible, from it.

Qadar, briefly, is that the timeless knowledge of God anticipates events, and events take place according to the exact knowledge of God. That is to say; events does not take place for Allah knows them, but He knows them for they will take place.

The Freedom of Individual

Every person is born free from sin. He is like a blank book. When the person reaches the age of puberty and maturity he becomes accountable for his deeds and intentions, if he is sane.

Man is not only free from sin until he commits sin, but he is also free to do things according to his plans on his own responsibility. This Islamic concept of freedom is based upon the principle of God's justice and the individual's direct responsibility to God. Each person must bear his own burden and be responsible for his own actions, because no one can expiate for another's sin.

To sum up, Islam is presented to mankind as a Divine formula for those who want to satisfy their moral and spiritual needs as well as their natural aspirations, those who want to lead a constructive and sound life, whether personal or social, national or international. The man is fully free to choose any of them and act accordingly. Only he may seek God's help for success.

CHAPTER THREE
THE WORSHIPS *('IBÂDÂT)*

SECTION ONE

THE MEANING OF WORSHIP *('İBÂDÂT)*

'İbâda is an arabic word derived from *'abd*. It means submission and servitude. Allah is your master and you are His slave. Whatever a slave does in obedience to and for the pleasure of his master is *'ibâda*.

The Islamic concept of *'ibâda* is very wide. All the activities of a muslim should be in accordance with the pleasure and consent of Allah.

To help achieve this aim, a set of formal worships have been drawn up as a course of training. The *'ibâdât* are thus the pillars on which the edifice of Islam rests. Any muslim who fails to observe his prayers and has no reasonable excuse is committing a grave offence and a sin. This offence is so grave because it is not only against God, but it is also against the very nature of man.

It should always be born in mind that God does not need man's prayer, because He is free of all needs. He is only interested in our responsibility and well-being in every sense. It is also a showing of gratituity to Allah for He created us and granted innumerable blessings and abundance.

Prophet Muhammad enjoined us to believe in five articles of Islam. He said: "Islam has been based on five fundamental principles. They are:

1- ***Kalima Shahâda;*** There is no deity but Allah and Muhammad is His servant and His Apostle.

2- Prayer *(salât)*

3- Alms *(zakât)*

4- Fasting *(sawm)*

5- Pilgrimage *(Hajj)*

The Categories Of Worship:

1- Physical worships; Prayer and fasting e.t.c.

2- Financial worships; The alms, sacrifice etc.

3- Both, physical and financial worships; Pilgrimage.

The Benefits of Worships

The benefits which can be derived from the Islamic worships are innumerable. Here are some:

1- They purify the heart and develope the mind, cultivate the conscience and comfort the soul.

2- Provide a safeguard against indecency and evil against wrong deviation and stray.

3- Demonstration of true equality, solid unity, and brotherhood.

4- An expression of thankfulness to God and appreciation of Him.

5- A course of inner peace and stability.

6- They are a unique satisfaction for the soul.

7- They have certain physical benefits. Such as physical purification and cleannes.

Who is legally Responsible *(mukallaf)* for worships?

In order to be held responsible for Divine obligations, a person should bear the following qualities.

1- Sanity

2- Maturity and puberty

According to Islam the age of puberty for girl is the age between; 9-15, for boys is between; 12-15.

It is an obligation of parents to teach their children before they are held responsible.

The Categories of Religious Commandments for Responsible Persons *(Ef'âl al-mukallafîn)*

1- *Fard* (imperative):

It is the act whose legal value ***(hukm)*** has been established by the Islamic evidence which there is no doubt about its *hukm*. Failure to belief in it entails unbelief ***(kufr),*** and failure to execute it causes impiety ***(fisq)***.

The *fard* is of two kinds:

a- *Fard 'ayn* (personal fard):

It is the act which every one must personally perform. The performance of the five daily prayers and the giving of *zakat* are of this kind.

b- *Fard Kifâya* (social fard):

It is the act which every person is under obligation to perform, until a sufficient number of persons have performed it. The rest being then absolved from the obligation. Examples of this obligation are the funeral prayer and holy war ***(jihâd)***.

2- *Wâjib* (obligatory):

It is the act whose *hukm* has been laid less strong than the ***fard*** by a Religious evidence. The examples can be given are: Prayers of ***'Îd,*** and sacrificing animal on the ***'Îd al-adha.*** The giving of ransom ***(fidya)*** for not fasting for some Religiously valid reasons.

The *hukm* of the *wajib* is that it must be executed like the fard. Although it need not be given absolute faith as the *fard*.

3- *Sunnat:* (1)

Practices exercised frequently by our Prophet. The acts which are not obligatory to the degree of being *fard* or *wâjib*,

(1) Sunnat in this sense must not be confused with sunnat in the sense of one of the four bases of fiqh.

and whose commission is still rewarded and is preferable to their omission, though does not entail Divine punishment.

The Kinds of *Sunnat*

a- *Sunnat al-muakkada:*

They are the acts that were performed by the Prophet habitually. Two *rek'ats* before the Morning Prayer, four *rek'ats* before and two *rek'ats* after the *fard* prayer in the Noon Prayer. Two *rek'ats* after *fard* in the Night Prayer.

b- *Sunnat ghayr muakkada:*

The prayers sometimes performed by the Prophet. Four *rek'ats* before the Afternoon Prayer *('asr),* and Night Prayer *('ishâ)* are of this type.

4- *Mustahab* (Recommendable):

The worships that the Prophet performed at one time and omitted at another time. Such as; supererogatory and extra prayers.

5- *Mubâh* (Indifferent):

It is the acts which a person is free to perform and whose is not rewarded and whose omission is no punished. Such as; sitting, and walking.

6- *Harâm* (Prohibited):

The strictly prohibited acts whose commission is punished, and omission is rewarded.

7- *Makrûh* is of two kinds:

a- *Karahat al-tahrîm* (Abominable to the degree of prohibition):

This kind is nearer to *harâm*. Commission is punished, omission is rewarded such as omission of *wâjibs*.

b- *Karahat al-tanzîh* (Abominable for the purpose of keeping pure):

This kind is nearer to the *mubâh*. Its ommission is not

punished but its commission is rewarded. Such as omission of *mustahâbs*.

Some Usefull Terminology:

Adâ: It is the performance of the obligation *('ayn)* at a time has been specified in the revealed sources.

Qadâ: It is the performance of a similar obligation in another time.

***I'ada* (repetition):** A second performance of an obligation at its set time. This done in the case when the first performance have been non-valid for some reasons.

***Niyat* (Intention):** The *niyat* is required before the performance of the *'ibâdât*, such as washing, prayer, alms, fasting, pilgrimage, sacrifice e.t.c. Without it they are not valid *(bâtıl)*. The decleration of *niyat* is pronounced orally or mentally.

SECTION TWO

PRAYER *(Salât)*

Prayer constitutes one pillar of Islam and considered the Foundation of Islam. *Negligence* of the prayer is a grave offence and a sin.

The Imperative *(Fard)* Prerequisites of the Prayer:

They are twelve; six of them are conditions ***(shart)*** which are performed before the prayer. Six of them are formal cause or pillars ***(rukn)*** which are performed during the prayer.

The conditions of the Prayer:

1- *Tahârat* from *Hadath* (ritual purity from ritual impurity):

To take *wudû* (ablution). If necessary to take ***ghusl*** (total ritual ablution) for cleansing from ***janabat***; a canonical impurity.

2- *Tahârat* from *Najâsat* (Purification from filth):

Purifying of the whole body, and the clothes worn on it, and the ground used for prayer from all kinds of dirt, such as blood, urine, excrement, wine, e.t.c.

3- *Satr al-'avrat* (Dressing up the Privy parts of the Body):

For Male: The body should be covered at least from the navel to the knees.

For Female: The whole body should be covered except the face, the hands and the feet.

For both, transparent clothes must be avoided in prayer.

4- *Istıqbâl al-Qıbla* (Facing the Right Direction):

The right direction for the prayer is the Ka'ba at Mecca.

5- *Waqt* (Prescribed Time):

Performing the prayers at their set up times.

6- *Niyat* (Intention):

Declaring the intention of prayer by heart. And pronounce it by tongue whenever possible, which is a *sunnat*.

The *Rukuns* of the Prayer:

1- *Takbîr al-iftitâh* (the opening *takbir*):

To start the prayer with (Allahu Akbar: Allah is Great)

2- *Qiyâm* (Upright Position):

3- *Qiraât* (Recitation):

To recite some verses from the Holy Qur'an while in the *qiyam*.

4- *Rukû'* (Bending):

Bowing in such a way that the palms of the hands reach the knees.

5- *Sajda* (Prostration):

The toes of both feet, hands, both knees, the nose, and the forehead should touch the ground.

6- *Qa'da* (Sitting):

Sitting at the end of the prayer for sometime sufficient for reciting the 'Attahiyyat' passage.

Missing any one of these twelve fard nullifies the prayer.

Rak'at (unit): A *rak'at* of the prayer consists of a *qiyâm*, a *ruku'*, and the *sajdas*.

The *Wâjibs* in the Prayer

1- To start the prayer with the phrase of *'Allah Akbar'*

2- Recitation of the *Sûra Fatiha* (chapter of opening) in the first two *rak'ats* of the four-*rak'at fard* prayers, and in the every *rak'at* of the ***nafl*** (supererogatory) prayers.

3- To recite some additional verses after the *Sûra Fâtiha* in the first two *rak'ats* of the fard prayers, in every *rak'ats* of the witr and nafl prayers.

4- Reciting the *Sûra Fâtiha* before the additional verses.

5- Performance of the two sajdas one after the other and touching the nose to the ground.

6- Performance of every *fard* as described, and while passing from one fard to the other, pausing for a while sufficient to pronounce the word *'subhanallah'*.

7- Sitting after the second *rak'at* in the three or four rak'at prayers. This is named 'first sitting' *(qa'da ûlâ)*.

8- The *imâm* (prayer leader) should recite the ***Fatiha*** and other additional verses aloud in every rak'at of the Morning (fajr), Friday, 'Îd, Tarawih, and Witr prayers.

And in the first two rak'ats of the Sunset *(maghrib)* and Night *('ishâ)* prayers when performed in congregation *(jama'at)*.

9- The followers praying in congregation must keep silent.

10- Recitation of *Qunût* in the *witr* prayer; both the imam and the followers should recite it in silence.

11- ***'Îd takbîrs;*** they are the six extra takbirs of *'Îd* prayers.

12- To end the prayers with *salâm* (greeting).

13- Performance of the ***'sajda sahw'*** (restoration sajda) in case some mistake is made during the prayer.

One *sahiv sajda* is sufficed for more than one mistakes.

The Cases cause *Sajda Sahiv:*

1- Disbanding or delaying the performance of any one of the *fards* in prayer.

2- Forgetting to perform or delaying any of the *wajibs* of the prayer.

How to Perform the *Sajda Sahw:*

As soon as teh first *salam* of the prayer is pronounced two extra *sajdas* are done as the usal ones. Then reciting the *Tahiyyât'* and *'Salawat'* while sitting. The prayer ends with *salâm* again.

In this way the missing part of the prayer is restored.

The *Sunnats* of the Prayer

1- Raising the hands to the ear level at the start of every prayer, and at the *Qunût takbîr* in the third *rak'at* of *Witr* prayer.

2- Reciting the *'Subhanaka'*, *'Aûdhu'* and *'Basmala'* at the beginning of the first *rak'at* of every prayer.

3- To say *'Âmîn'* silently after the recitation of the Sûra Fâtiha in the prayers performed both individually all in congregation.

4- To utter all other *takbîrs* along with the opening ***takbir***.

5- To say ***'sami'a Allah liman hamidah'***, ***'Rabbanâ lakal hamd'*** after repositioned from the *rukû'*.

6- Repeating three times the 'Subhâne Rabbi al-'azîm' in the *rukû*, and the ***'Subhâne Rabbi al-a'lâ*** in the *sajda*.

7- In the ***ruku'***, capping the knees with the palms of the hands and keeping the fingers aprt and holding the knees. The elbows to be straight whereas the back and the head are in horizontal position.

The ladies keep the fingers sticked together, do not hold the knees. Only they put their palms on.

8- In the *sajda*, first the knees and hands, then the forehead should be placed on the ground. Positioning the forehead in between the hands. To raise from the *sajda;* first the forehead, then the hands and after, the knees will be lifted.

9- Recitation of the *'Tahiyyât'* silently while placing the hands on the knees in the sitting. The recitation of *'Salawat'* and the prescribed prayer.

10- At the end of the prayer; turning the head to the right first and saying; ***'Assalâmu 'alaykum wa rahmatullah',*** and turning to the left and repeating the same phrase.

The *Mandûbs* of the *Salât:*

1- To look at the *sajda* point while standing up.

2- To look at the feet while in the *rukû'*.

3- To look at the lap while sitting.

4- To look over the shoulders while uttering the *salam*.

5- To look at the sides of the nose while in the *sajda*.

The Abominables of the *Salât*:

1- To play with any part of the body, yawning and stretching.

2- To stand in prayer with improper clothes and sleeves rolled up, and sitting improperly.

3- To close or to raise the eyes in the prayer; to divert the head from the *qıbla*.

4- In congregational prayer, to stand apart while there is a vacuum in the front row. To stand for prayer in front of a burning fire, a picture or a humanbeing.

5- Omission any of the *sunnats* of the prayer.

The Deeds invalidate the Prayer:

1- Speaking, laughing, eating, greating, deliberate coughing, blowing, sleeping, leaning against something, and mormuring as of, pof e.t.c. during the prayer.

2- Omitting any of the *fards* of the prayer.

3- Performance of the prayer in line with man and woman without a screen or curtain or a partition in between.

4- Exposing the private parts of the body for a duration of one ***rukn*** (one principle of the prayer).

5- Reciting the Qur'an from the Book.

6- Rasing of the Sun while performing the Morning Prayer.

7- To shift the position from the *qıbla*.

8- To do anything that nullifies the ablution.

PRAYER *(SALÂT)* GUIDE

The Prayer Call *(Adhân)*

When the time of prayer comes, it is required to call ***adhân***. The caller stands facing the ***qibla,*** raising both hands to the ears and says, in a loud voice, the following:

1- ***Allâhu Akbar:***

الله اكبر

Allah is the Greatest.
(repeated four times)

2- ***Ashhadu an-lâilâhe illallâh:***

اشهد ان لا اله إلا الله

I bear witness that there is no god but Allah.
(repeated twice)

3- ***Ashhadu anna Muhammadar Rasulullah:***

اشهد ان محمداً رسول الله

I bear witness that Muhammad is the Messenger of Allah.
(repeated twice)

4- ***Hayya 'alas Salâh:***

حى على الصلاة

Come fast to prayer.
(repeated twice, and turning the face to the right)

5- ***Hayya 'alal Falâh:***

حى على الفلاح

Come fast to the salvation
(repeated twice, and turning the face to the left)

6- ***Allâhu Akbar:***

الله اكبر

God is the Greatest
(repeated twice)

7- *Lâilâhe illallâh:*

لا اله الا الله

There is no god but Allah
(once)

When the call is made for the Morning Prayer ***(Fajr)***, the caller adds one sentence right after part (5) above. The sentence is:

Assalât Khayrun mina'n Nawm:

الصلاة خير من النوم

(repeated twice)
Prayer is better than the sleep.

Entrance into Prayer *(ıqâmat)*

For inaugurating the *fard* prayer this call is uttered. The sentences here are the same as those of the *adhân* with two differences.

a- The *ıqâmat* is said in a faster and less audible voice.

b- Right after part (5), the sentence;

قد قامت الصلاة

qad qâmat as salat: prayer is ready
(repeated twice)

THE ILLUSTRATED PERFORMANCE OF PRAYER

UNIT ONE

THE MORNING PRAYER *(SALÂT AL-FAJR)*

This prayer consists of: *a- sunnat;* two rak'ats. *b- fard;* two rak'ats.

There is no difference between the *sunnat* and the fard, except that when declaring the intention, one has to distinguish between the two kinds. Therefore as an example the fard has been described with illustration.

1- The Performance of the *Fard*:

Niyat: I intended, for the sake of God, to perform today's Morning Prayer's fard.

نويت ان اصلى فرض صلاة الفجر رضاء لله

Transliteration: Nawaytu an usalliya fard salat al-Fajr, rıdaen lillah.

1- Saying the takbir iftitah: *Allahu Akbar* الله اكبر

Figure: 1 (Males)
As saying the ***takbîr***; the palms should face the ***qıbla***. The thumbs should be raised up to the ears.

Figure: 2 (Females)
As saying the ***takbîr***; the palms should face the ***qıbla***. The arms raised as the finger tips reach the shoulders.

2- *Qıyâm:* The standing up

Figure: 3 (Males)
Lowering the arms and placing the right hand over the left one, right below the navel.

Figure: 4 (Females)
Lowering the arms and placing the right hand over the left one, right over the chest.

Then saying in a low voice:

a- the ***Subhânaka***, which is:

سُبْحَانَكَ اللّٰهُمَّ وَبِحَمْدِكَ وَتَبَارَكَ اسْمُكَ وَتَعَالٰى
جَدُّكَ (وَجَلَّ ثَنَاۤؤُكَ) وَلَاۤ اِلٰهَ غَيْرُكَ

Transliteration:

Subhanakallahumma wa bi hamdik, wa tabarakasmuk, wa ta'ala jadduk, wa la ilaha Ghayruk.

Translation:

"Glory be to You, O God, and Yours is the praise, and blessed is Your name, and exalted is Your majesty, and there is no god besides You.

b- the ***A'ûdhu-Basmala***, which is:

اعوذ بالله من الشيطان الرجيم

Transliteration:

A'ûdhu billâhi mina'sh shaytâni'r rajîm.
Bismillâhi'r Rahmâni'r Rahîm.

بسم الله الرحمن الرحيم

Translation:

I seek the refuge of God from the condemned devil.
In the name of God, Most Gracious, Most Merciful.

c- the Sûra Fâtiha (the Opening Chapter), which is:

بِسْمِ اللّٰهِ الرَّحْمٰنِ الرَّحِيمِ

اَلْحَمْدُ لِلّٰهِ رَبِّ الْعَالَمِينَ ۝ اَلرَّحْمٰنِ الرَّحِيمِ ۝ مَالِكِ
يَوْمِ الدِّينِ ۝ اِيَّاكَ نَعْبُدُ وَاِيَّاكَ نَسْتَعِينُ ۝ اِهْدِنَا
الصِّرَاطَ الْمُسْتَقِيمَ ۝ صِرَاطَ الَّذِينَ اَنْعَمْتَ عَلَيْهِمْ
غَيْرِ الْمَغْضُوبِ عَلَيْهِمْ وَلَا الضَّالِّينَ ۝

Transliteration:

Alhamdu lillâhi Rabbi'l 'Âlemîn. Ar rahmâni'r rahîm. Mâliki yawmid dîn. Iyyâke na'budu wa iyyâ ke nasta'în. Ihdinas Sırâtal mustakîm, Sırâtalladhîna an'amta 'alayhim, ghayril maghdûbi 'alayhim wa laddâllîn.

d- Some verses of Qur'an or a small additional sûra, for example;

the Sûra, 'asr, which is:

و العصر ان الانسان لفى خسر الا الذين آمنوا
وعملوا الصالحات وتوا صوا بالحق وتوا صوا بالصبر

Transliteration:

Wal 'asr innal insâna la fî khusr, illalladhîna âmanû wa 'amilü's sâlihât wa tawâsaw bilhaqqı watawâsaw bissabr.

Then saying: ***Allâhu Akbar***, for ***rukû'***.

3- *Rukû:* The Bending

In the *ruku'*, saying in a low voice:

سبحان ربى العظيم

Transliteration:

Subhâna Rabbiya'l 'adhîm (repeated three times)

Translation:

Glory be to my Lord the Great.

Figure: 5 (Males)
Lowering the head down at a right angle. Placing the palms of the hands on the knees. The arms and the back should be stretched.

Figure: 6 (Females)
The females' back should be curved. Bending less than the males. Placing the palms on the knees and saying the same phrase.

To resume from the ***rukû'***, saying:

سمع الله لمن حمده

Transliteration:

Sami'allahu Liman Hamidah

Translation:

God accepts any who are thankful to Him.

When saying this the hands remain on the sides.

Figure: 7

Figure: 8

For going to the *sajda*; saying: ***Allahu Akbar***

الله اكبر

4- *Sajda:* Prostration

In going to *sajda*; first the knees, then hands, after, forehead and nose should touch the ground. The head should be positioned between the hands. Here saying:

سبحان ربى الاعلى

Transliteration:

Subhâna Rabbiya'l A'lâ (repeated three times)

Translation:

Glory to my Lord the Most High

Figure: 9 (Males)

The elbowes should be a little bit away of the body, and the arms lifted up. The toes should face tha ***qıbla.***

Figure: 10 (Females)

The ladies' arms should touch to the sides and the elbows to the ground.

Then with the utterance of *Allahu Akbar* resuming from the first *sajda.* Then comes the *jalsa.*

5- *Jalsa:* Short Sitting Posture

Figure: 11 (Males)

Figure: 12 (Females)

Figure: 11 (Males)

The outer side of the left foot and the toes of the right one, which are in erect position directed to *qıbla,* touching the ground and the two hands are placed on two knees.

Figure: 12 (Females)

The feet should be leaning towards the right side. They should not be erected.

6- Second *Sajda*

With the utterance of ***Allahu Akbar*** the prostration is repeated in the same way with the same utterances as in the first one.

With these actions the first *rukûn* (unit) of the prayer is completed.

After the first unit the worshipper rises saying. ***Allahu Akbar*** to assume a standing position for the second unit.

Second *sajda* for males

Figure: 13

Second *sajda* for females

Figure: 14

The Second *Rak'at*

1- In the *qıyam:*

a- *Basmala*

b- the *Sûra Fâtiha*

c- Additional Qur'anic passage

are recited as in the first unit.

the *qıyâm* of the males

Figure: 15

the *qıyâm* of the females

Figure: 16

2- Carrying out the *rak'at* as it was in the first unit.

the *rukû'* of males

Figure: 17

the *rukû'* of females

Figure: 18

3- When the two prostrations are finished, the *qa'da âkhira* is fulfilled.

7- *Qa'da Âkhira* (Final Sitting)

It is a sitting position as in the *jalsa*,

with the utterance of ***Allahu Akbar,*** raising from the *sajda*, and sitting.

Figure: 19 - 20 (Males)

The males leaning the foot and sitting on it. The toes of the right foot erected and directed to ***qibla.***

Figure: 21 (Females)

They lean both feet towards the rights side and sit.

and reciting;

a- the Tahiyyât, which is:

اَلتَّحِيَّاتُ لِلّٰهِ وَالصَّلَوَاتُ وَالطَّيِّبَاتُ اَلسَّلَامُ عَلَيْكَ
اَيُّهَا النَّبِيُّ وَرَحْمَةُ اللّٰهِ وَبَرَكَاتُهُ اَلسَّلَامُ عَلَيْنَا
وَعَلٰى عِبَادِ اللّٰهِ الصَّالِحِينَ اَشْهَدُ اَنْ لَا اِلٰهَ اِلَّا اللّٰهُ
وَاَشْهَدُ اَنَّ مُحَمَّدًا عَبْدُهُ وَرَسُولُهُ

Transliteration:

Attahiyyatu lillâhi wassalawât, wattayyibât. Assalâmu 'alayka ayyuhan Nabiyyu wa rahmatullahi wa barakâtuh. Assalamu 'alayna, wa 'alâ 'ibâdillahis Sâlihîn.

Ashhadu an lâ ilâha illallâh. Wa ashhadu anna Muhammadan 'abduhu wa rasûluh.

Translation:

All reverence, all worship, all sanctity are due to God. Salam (Peace) be on you, O Prophet, and the mercy of God and His blessings.

Peace be upon us all and on the righteous servants of God. I bear witness that there is no god but Allah alone, and I bear witness that Muhammad is His servant and His Messenger.

b- the *Salâwâts,* which are:

اَللّٰهُمَّ صَلِّ عَلٰى مُحَمَّدٍ وَعَلٰى اٰلِ مُحَمَّدٍ كَمَا صَلَّيْتَ عَلٰى
اِبْرَاهِيمَ وَعَلٰى اٰلِ اِبْرَاهِيمَ اِنَّكَ حَمِيدٌ مَجِيدٌ

اَللّٰهُمَّ بَارِكْ عَلٰى مُحَمَّدٍ وَعَلٰى اٰلِ مُحَمَّدٍ كَمَا بَارَكْتَ
عَلٰى اِبْرَاهِيمَ وَعَلٰى اٰلِ اِبْرَاهِيمَ اِنَّكَ حَمِيدٌ مَجِيدٌ

Transliteration:

Allahumma salli 'alâ muhammad, wa 'alâ âli Muhammad. Kama sallayta 'alâ sayyidinâ Ibrahîm wa 'âla âli Ibrahîm. Innaka Hamîdun Majîd.

Allahumma bârik 'alâ Muhammad, wa 'alâ âli Muhammad. kamâ barakta 'alâ Ibrahim. Wa 'alâ âli Ibrahîm. Innaka Hamîdun Majîd.

Translation:

a- O my God! Exalt Muhammad and the family of Muhammad, as You did exalt Abraham and the family of Abraham. Verily You are Praiseworthy and Glorious.

b- O my God! Bless Muhammad and the family of Muhammad, as You did bless Abraham, and the family of Abraham. Verily You are Praiseworthy and Glorious.

c- **The Prays**, which are:

رَبَّنَا آتِنَا فِي الدُّنْيَا حَسَنَةً وَفِي الْآخِرَةِ حَسَنَةً وَقِنَا
عَذَابَ النَّارِ رَبَّنَا اغْفِرْ لِي وَلِوَالِدَيَّ وَلِلْمُؤْمِنِينَ
يَوْمَ يَقُومُ الْحِسَابُ بِرَحْمَتِكَ يَا أَرْحَمَ الرَّاحِمِينَ

Transliteration:

Rabbana âtinâ fid Dunyâ hasanatan, wa fil âkhirati hasanatan, wa qınâ adhâban Nâr, bi Rahmatika yâ arhamar Râhimîn.

Rabbanaghfirly wa li walidayya wa lil mu'mınîn yawma yaqûmul hisâb.

Translation:

O my God! Give us the goodness in this world and in the Next, and save us from the Hell, with Your affection, the Most Affectionate off all.

O my God! Forgive my sins and those of my parents and of the believers, when the Day of Judgement comes.

5- *Salâm* (Greeting):

a- *Salâm* to the right

The males and the females turn the face to the right side saying:

Assalâmu 'alaykum wa rahmatullah

(Peace be on you and the mercy of God)

Figure: 22

Figure: 23

b- *Salâm* to the left

Turning the face to the left side uttering the same greeting.

Figure: 24

Figure: 25

6- *Du'a* (Pray)

Following the completion of *salat* a pray is rendered.

The style of the *du'a* for both the males and females have been illustrated in figures 26 and 27.

Figure: 26 (Males)

Figure: 27 (Females)

This is how any prayer of two units, whether *fard* or *sunnat* is performed. When knowing how to perform this prayer in the right way, all other prayers will be found very easy.

It should be point out that every move or every word in the Islamic prayer has a great significance attached to it and is symbolic of a very deep meaning.

UNIT TWO

THE NOON PRAYER *(SALAT ZUHR)*

This consists of;

a- four rak'ats as the first *sunnat*

b- four rak'ats as the *fard*

c- two rak'ats as the last *sunnat*.

The Performance of the *sunnat* of this prayer is as follows:

a- The first two rak'ats are performed in the same way as described in the morning prayer. At the first *qa'da* stop the recitation of the salawats and prays, because this sitting is the first sitting ***(qa'da ûlâ).*** Only in the last sittings they are recited. Without greetings raised for the third *rak'at.*

b- The third and the fourth *rak'ats* are performed in the same way, but without reciting the *subhanaka.*

c- At the end of fourth *rak'at,* the procedure of the *qa'da, âkhıra* is fulfilled.

In this way the *sunnat* is concluded.

The Performance of the last *sunnat*

It is performed in the same way as its *sunnat,* with one difference, in the third and fourth *rak'ats* no additional recitation is made after the ***sûra Fâtiha***.

The Performance of the last *sunnat*

It is performed in the same way as the fard of Morning Prayer.

UNIT THREE

THE MID-AFTERNOON PRAYER *(SALAT 'ASR)*

It consists of:

a- four *rak'ats* of first *sunnat*

b- four *rak'ats* of *fard*

The Performance of the *sunnat*

Its performance is exactly in the same way as the *sunnat* of the noon prayer. With two exceptions; reciting prayers at the first *qa'da* and *basmala* at the beginning of the third *rak'at.*

The performance of the fard

It is performed in the same way as the *fard* of the noon prayer.

UNIT FOUR

THE SUNSET PRAYER *(SALAT MAGHRIB)*

This consists of:

a- three *rak'ats* of *fard*, and followed by

b- two *rak'ats* of *sunnat*

The Performance of the *fard*

The first two *rak'ats* are performed in the same way as the first two *rak'ats* of the *fard* of noon prayer. And the third *rak'at* is performed as the last *rak'at* of the fard of the noon prayer.

The Performance of the *sunnat*

It is performed in the same way as described in the *fard* of the morning prayer.

UNIT FIVE

THE EVENING PRAYER *(SALAT 'ÎSHÂ)*

It consists of:

a- four *rak'ats* of the first *sunnat*, and followed by

b- four *rak'ats* of the *fard*, and followed by

c- two *rak'ats* of the last *sunnat*, and followed by

d- three *rak'ats* of *salat witr*

The Performance

The first *sunnat* is performed in the same way as the *sunnat* of the ***salat 'asr.***

The ***fard*** is performed in the same way as the *fard* of the ***salat fajr***.

The first two *rak'ats* of the *witr* is performed just like the first two *rak'ats* of the *sunnat* of the noon prayer.

The third *rak'at* is performed as follows.

When completing the first two *rak'ats* without greetings standing up and reciting:

a- *basmala*

b- fâtiha

c- passage from the Qur'an, then saying ***Allahu Akbar*** and raising the hands up to the ears.

Then placing the hands in the usal way.

After that reciting the ***Qunût Pray***, which is :

اَللّٰهُمَّ اِنَّا نَسْتَعِينُكَ وَنَسْتَغْفِرُكَ وَنَسْتَهْدِيكَ

وَنُؤْمِنُ بِكَ وَنَتُوبُ اِلَيْكَ وَنَتَوَكَّلُ عَلَيْكَ وَنُثْنِى

عَلَيْكَ الْخَيْرَ كُلَّهُ نَشْكُرُكَ وَلَا نَكْفُرُكَ

وَنَخْلَعُ وَنَتْرُكُ مَنْ يَفْجُرُكَ

اَللّٰهُمَّ اِيَّاكَ نَعْبُدُ وَلَكَ نُصَلِّى وَنَسْجُدُ وَاِلَيْكَ نَسْعٰى

وَنَحْفِدُ نَرْجُو رَحْمَتَكَ وَنَخْشٰى عَذَابَكَ اِنَّ عَذَابَكَ

بِالْكُفَّارِ مُلْحِقٌ

Transliteration:

Allahumma innâ nasta'înuka wa nastaghfiruka, wa nastahdîka, wa nu'minu bika, wa natûbu ilayka, wa natawakkalu 'alayka, wa nuthnî 'alayka'l khayra kullahu. Nashkuruka wa la nakfuruka. Wa nakhla'u wa natruku man yafjuruka.

Allahumma iyyaka na'budu wa laka nusallî wa nasjudu. Wa ilayka nas'a wa nakhfidu. Narjû rahmataka. Wa nakhshâ 'adhabaka. Inna 'adhabaka bil kuffari mulhıq.

Translation:

O my God! We beseech You for help and forgiveness, and guidance. We believe in You and seek your protection, and rely on You. And we extol you and are thankful to You and not ingrate to You. We declare ourselves clearof, and forsake, him who disobeys You.

O God! To You do we pray and prostrate ourselves. To obey You we are quick, and Your mercy do we hope for and Your punishment do we fear. For Your punishment overtakes the unbelievers.

All the prayers must be clearly stated in the *niyat* before the performance.

In every prayer performed individually, all the utterances and the recitations should be made in silence. If they are performed in congretation the *imâm* (prayer leader) should make the recitations aloud, where necessary, and the utterances in an audible voice.

The *sunnats* are not to be made up *(qadâ)* if they are missed. They are performed at their prescribed time. Instead the missed fards are to be made up.

The Supplications *(Du'â)* After the Prayer

Allahumma antas salam wa minkas salam tabarakta ya dhal jalâl wal ikrâm.

b- ***Ayat al-Kursî*** (Throne Verse):

بِسْمِ اللهِ الرَّحْمٰنِ الرَّحِيمِ

اَللّٰهُ لَآ اِلٰهَ اِلَّا هُوَ اَلْحَيُّ الْقَيُّومُ لَا تَأْخُذُهُ سِنَةٌ وَلَا نَوْمٌ لَهُ مَا

فِي السَّمٰوَاتِ وَمَا فِي الْاَرْضِ مَنْ ذَا الَّذِي يَشْفَعُ عِنْدَهُ اِلَّا بِاِذْنِهِ

يَعْلَمُ مَا بَيْنَ اَيْدِيهِمْ وَمَا خَلْفَهُمْ وَلَا يُحِيطُونَ بِشَيْءٍ مِنْ

عِلْمِهِ اِلَّا بِمَا شَاءَ وَسِعَ كُرْسِيُّهُ السَّمٰوَاتِ وَالْاَرْضَ

وَلَا يَؤُدُهُ حِفْظُهُمَا وَهُوَ الْعَلِيُّ الْعَظِيمُ ۝

Transliteration:

Allâhu lâ ilâha illâ huwa al-hayyul Qayyûm. Lâ ta'khudhuhu sinatun wa lâ nawm. Lahu mâ fis samawât wa mâ fil ard. Man dhalladhî yashfa'u 'indahu illâ bi idhnih. Ya'lamu ma bayna aydihim wa mâ khalfahum. Wa lâ yuhîtuna bi shayin min 'ilmih, illâ bi mâ shâa. Wasi'a kursiyyuhus samawât wal ard. Wa lâ yaûduhu hıfzuhuma, wa huwal 'aliyyul 'azım.

The ***Tasbîh:***

33 times ***Subhanallah*** سبحان الله

33 times ***Alhamdulillah*** الحمد لله

33 times ***Allahu Akbar*** الله اكبر

After that:

لَآ إِلٰهَ إِلَّا اللّٰهُ وَحْدَهُ لَا شَرِيكَ لَهُ، لَهُ الْمُلْكُ وَلَهُ الْحَمْدُ

وَهُوَ عَلٰى كُلِّ شَيْءٍ قَدِيرٌ

Lailâha illâllâhu wahdahu lâ sharîkalahu lahul mulk wa lahul hamd, wa huwa 'alâ kullî shayin qadîr. Subhana Rabbiyal 'aliyyil a'lal wahhab. Then the pray is made.

Now the prayer is concluded.

How a Sick Person Performs the Prayer?

There is no hardship in Islam, therefore who cannot perform the prayer in legally described form, it is allowed to fulfil it in convenience. When one is so sick that unable to stand up performing the prayer by sitting is allowed. If cannot sit, he can perform it by leaning against a wall. Those who are unable to make *rukû'* and *sajda* may perform them by gesture: They bow slightly for *ruku'* and a little more for *sajda.*

If unable to those activities, he is allowed to perform the prayer by lying on the bed however is convenient.

UNIT SIX

THE FRIDAY PRAYER *(SALÂT AL-JUM'A)*

So far we have been dealing with daily prayers. Now we come to the weekly convention of Friday Congregation.

Who are obliged with the *Cum'a* prayer?

This prayer is compalsory upon every male, adult ***(bâligh),*** sane ***('âqıl),*** free ***(hur),*** legally considered resident in the locality ***(muqîm)*** and physically fit Muslim.

The Conditions for the Validity of *Jum'a* Prayer

1- It should be at the time of the noon prayer on Friday

2- There should be a ***Khutba*** (sermon) preceded the prayer.

3- There should be three persons besides ımâm.

The Performance of the Prayer

It consists of:

a- four *rak'ats* of first *sunnat*

b- two *rak'ats* of *fard*

c- four rak'ats of the last *sunnat*

The four rak'ats of first *sunnat* is performed exactly in the same way as the first *sunnat* of the *zuhr* prayer.

Then an inner *adhân* is called inside the mosque.

The imam stands up facing the audience and delivers his sermon, which is an essential part of the prayer. While the *imâm* is delivering the *khutba* nobody should talk or pray, but listen to the sermon. After the conclusion of the sermon the *iqâmat* is made and two *rak'ats* of obligatory prayer is offered under the leadership of the *imâm*. After that, four *rak'ats* of last *sunnat* is performed individually. It should be pointed out that all the *sunnat* prayers are performed individually.

This prayer must be performed in congregation led by an *imâm*. It cannot be offered individually on ones own. If any person mises it, he cannot make it up. Instead he has to offer the noon prayer.

All kinds of normal work are allowed on Friday as on any other week day. After the service is over, the people may resume their mundane activities.

The *jum'a* prayer substitutes the *salat zuhr* at the same time. Therefore make up is not required.

UNIT SEVEN

THE *TARAWÎH* PRAYERS

These prayers are special to the month of ***Ramadân***. They follow the Evening Prayer ***('Îshâ)***. They consist of eight to twenty *rak'ats* offered two by two with a short break in between. It is much more preferable to perform them in congregational form and before the *Witr*.

They are performed exactly in the same way as the morning prayer.

UNIT EIGHT

THE *'ÎD* (CANONICAL FESTIVAL) PRAYERS

There are two ***'Îd*** prayers in a year. One is on the ***'Îd al-Fitr*** (breaking the fast) day, and the other one is on the day of ***'Id al-Adhâ*** (sacrifice). These are considered *wâjib* prayers.

The time of this prayer is any time after sunrise and before noon. No *adhân* or *iqâmat* is required.

The prayer consists of two *rak'ats*. It must be performed in congregation led by an *imâm*. There is no substitute for it if missed.

The Performance of the Prayer

This prayer is slightly different from other prayers.

The *imâm* declares his intention to lead the prayer and saying ***Allahu Akbar (Takbîr)***. Then the *subhanaka* is recited. After that he says Allahu Akbar, and he repeats the same uttering three times. Rising his hands up to the ears and dropping them by his sides at the end of each utterence. On the completion of the third *takbîr* he places the right hand over the left one under the navel as in the other prayers. Then the *fâtiha* and a Qur'anic passage are recited by the *imâm* aloud. With bowing and prostration, the first unit is completed.

The worshippers follow the *imâm* in these movements step by step, doing and saying exactly the same.

At the end of the first unit, the *imâm* raises up for the second, saying ***Allahu Akbar.*** Then reciting *sûra Fâtiha* and a Qur'anic passage, then he adds three *takbîrs* as he did in the first *rak'at.* After that, *rukû'* and the other parts completed as in usual prayer.

Then the *imâm* delivers a ***khutba.*** In the sermon of the *'Îd al Fitr* he draws attention to the matter of *sadaqat al-Fitr.* This is an obligatory donation, whereby every individual Muslim who can afford it must give at least one full meal, or its value, to the poort. If he has any dependents, he must pay the same amount for each of them. This charity is far more rewarding and preferable if it is distributed early enough before the prayer so that the poor may be able to receive the Day in a festive and cheerful spirit.

It should be noted that these prayers are *wajib.* But they do not substitute the obligatory *fajr* prayer.

The *Takbîr Tashrîq*

Starting after the ***fajr*** prayer on the Eve and up to the *'asr* prayer of the fourth day of the *Îd Adhâ.*

The Takbir is as follows:

الله اكبر لااله الا الله والله اكبر الله اكبر و لله الحمد

Transliteration:

Allâhu Akbar, Allâhu Akbar, Lâ ilâha illallâhu wallâhu Akbar, Allâhu Akbar wa lillâhil hamd.

The utterance of this takbir at the described time is *wajib.* Who make up the missed prayers in a later time he should make them up as well.

UNIT NINE

THE TRAVELLER'S PRAYER *(SALÂT AL-MUSÂFIR)*

When a person is travelling with the intention of travelling ninety kilometers or over from his home he should shorten the obligatory *(fard)* prayers of four *rak'ats* to two each. The *fajr* and the *maghrib* prayers remain unchanged.

This advantage remains effective after the traveller arrives at his destination, if he does not intend to prolong his stay there for fifteen days or more.

The traveller when he returns back to his home, he makes up the missed prayers as two *rak'ats.*

Times When Prayer is Forbidden

1- The time when the sun is rising

2- The time when the sun is at ts Zenith

3- The time when the sun is setting

4- The period of menstruation and pueperium

5- The time of canonical impurity (janabat).

The Make Up for Missed Prayers *(Qadâ)*

As a rule, every Muslim, male or female, should offer the prayer in its due time. Failing to do so is a punishable sin unless there is a reasonable excuse.

With the exception of women in confinement or menstruation and any who remains insane or unconscious for some time, every Muslim must make up for the missed obligatory prayers.

When making up the prayers one must offer them in their original form, e.g., if they were shortened they should be offered so and vice-versa.

For every prayer to be made up. *iqâmat* is required. Not for the *witr* prayer.

UNIT TEN

THE FUNERAL PRAYER *(SALÂT AL-JANÂZA)*

The prayer to God for the deceased Muslim is a collective duty ***(fard Kifâya)***. This means that some Muslims should offer this prayer, and when it is offered by some of the muslims present at the time, it is sufficient, and the other Muslims become exempt from responsibility.

The dead body is placed on a bier or in a coffin and carried to the place of prayer. The coffin is put in a position that the dead's face direct towards *qıbla.*

The Performance of the Prayer

The imam stands beside the body facing the *qıbla* with the followers in line behind him. The imam rasing the hands to the ears with the decleration of intention, to pray to God for that particular deceased one. And saying ***Allâhu Akbar***. The worshippers follow the imam's lead and after him place their right hands over the left ones under the navel as in other prayers.

Then the imam recites in slience; the ***subhânaka*** with the addition of ***'wa jalla thanâuk'*** before the sentence of ***'wa la ilâha ghayruk'.***

Then the sûra fâtiha only. At this stage he says ***Allâhu Akbar*** without rasing the hands, and offer his suplication ***(Du'â)*** in any suitable words he knows, preferably these:

اَللّٰهُمَّ اغْفِرْ لِحَيِّنَا وَمَيِّتِنَا وَشَاهِدِنَا وَغَائِبِنَا وَذَكَرِنَا
وَأُنْثَانَا وَصَغِيرِنَا وَكَبِيرِنَا

اَللّٰهُمَّ مَنْ اَحْيَيْتَهُ مِنَّا فَاَحْيِهِ عَلَى الْاِسْلَامِ وَمَنْ
تَوَفَّيْتَهُ مِنَّا فَتَوَفَّهُ عَلَى الْاِيمَانِ

Transliteration:

Allahummaghfir li hayyina wa mayyitina wa shahidina wa ghaibina wa dhakarina wa unthana. Allahumma man ahyaytahu minna fa ahyihi 'alal Islami wa man tawaffaytahu minna fa tawaffahu 'alal iman.

Then the fourth takbir is said without raising the hands followed by the concluding greetings *(salam)* right and left as in other prayers. The worshippers follow the imam step by step and recite privately the same utterances silently. In this way the prayer has been completed.

UNIT ELEVEN

THE CONGREGATIONAL (JAMÂ'AT) PRAYERS

Whenever there is on opportunity for praying in congregation, a Muslim should not miss it, and it is twentyseven times more rewardable than a prayer performed in solo.

Prayer is a demonstration of unity in purpose and action, of purely piety and humility before God. And of effective solidarity among Muslims, of public order and mutual response.

The congregation is led by a prayer leader, called imam. He stands in the front alone, while the followers stand behind him in straight lines, all facing the *qibla.* A congregation can be made up of even two persons: the imam and one follower.

The imam declares the intention stating that he is leading the *salât* of who is following him. The followers, at the same time, make intention, stating that he is following the imam. The imam makes the recitings aloud in the two *rak'ats* of the *fajr* prayer, and the first two units of the *maghrib* and *'ishâ* prayers. When the imam is reciting, the followers keep silent. They do not recite the *Fâtiha* nor the other passage after the imam.

When the imam concludes the ***Fâtiha***, the followers say ***'Âmîn'.*** After the imam resumes from the ruku' (bowing) posture he says: *"sami'allâhu liman hamidah"*, and the follower responds in these words: *"Rabbana lakal hamd."*

The followers should follow the imam in his movements without preceding him in any act. Should any follower supercede the imam in any movement, this person's prayer will become void.

If a person comes after the start of the prayer and joins the congregation, he must, even if he has missed one unit or more, follow the imam. When the imam completes the service by uttering the final greeting, this late comer does not join in that, but takes a standing position to make up for the early units he missed.

When the person joints the congregation in the *rukû'* position, before raising, he is considered as having joined from the start of this particular unit. But if he joins in any position after raising from *rukû'* he has missed the unit and must make up for it individually right after the imam concludes the prayer.

SECTION THREE

ABLUTION

For a religiously valid *salât*, ablution *(wudû')* is *fard* precondition. Without it, the *salat* is not sufficed. Our Prophet Muhammad has said : *"The key of the salât is the wudû"*. (Al-Jami' Al- Saghîr, v.2, pp.156.

The *Fards* of the *Wudû'* :

1- Washing the whole face, from the top of the forehead to the bottom of the chin and from ear to ear, once.

2- Washing the arms up to the elbows, once.

3- Wiping the top part of the head with wet riht hand palm.

4- Washing the feet up to the ankle, once.

The *Sunnats* of the *Wudû':*

1- Decleration of the intention *(niyat)* for *wudû'*.

2- Saying the ***'Aûdhu Basmala'***.

3- Rinsing out the mouth and cleansing the nostrils by sniffing water into.

4- Following the sequence.

5- Starting with the right side.

6- Wiping the ears and the neck with wet hands.

7- Brushing the teeth.

8- Making the washings and the rinsings three times.

The *Makrûhs* of *Wudû:*

1- to be extravagant in using the water.

2- Using insufficient water.

3- Splashing the water.

4- Taking *wudû'* in a dirty place.

The Spoilers of the *Wudû:*

1- Natural discharges, i.e., urination, defecation, and breaking wind.

2- Flow of blood, pus or yellow water from the wounds.

3- Vomiting of a mouthfull.

4- Sleeping on a bed or by leaning against anything.

5- Fainting.

6- Drunkness.

Any of these occure, *wudû'* must be renewed for prayer.

Tears, blood and pus which do not spread around, do not spoil the *wudû'*.

***Wudû'* is required for the followings:**

1- *Salât*

2- Touching to the Kur'ân

3- *Sajda Tilâwat*

4- Circummambulation *(Tawâf)* to Ka'ba.

5- Funeral Prayer.

For performance of anyone of these the *wudû'* is required.

THE EXCUSED PERSON *(SÂHIB AL-'UDHR)*

Those who have durable deficiencies such as; nose bleeding, urine flowing, troubled eyes and ears which are of the spoilers of the *wudû'*, are considered excused. Those may perform prayers even if these excuses continue, provided they take ablution for every prayer.

ILLUSTRATED ABLUTION GUIDE

Figure: 1

First roll up the sleeves up to the elbows. Then declare the intention: "For the pleasure of God I intended to take ablution". Then say: ***Aûdhu billahi min ashshaytanırrajim, Bismillahirrahmanirrahim.*** (This is briefly called ***'Audhu Basmala').***

Figure: 2

Wash the hands up to the wrists, three times.

Figure: 3

Take water into the mouth with the right hand palm, and rins it, three times.

Figure: 4

Sniff water into the nostrils, using the right hand palm, three times.

Expel the water with the left hand.

Figure: 4

Figure: 5

Figure: 5

Wash the whole face with both hands, from the top of the forehead to the bottom of the chin and from the ear to ear, three times.

Figure: 6

Wash the right arm up to the far end of the elbow, three times.

Figure: 7

Wash the left arm up to the far end of the elbow, three times.

Figure: 8

Wipe at least the quarter of the head with wet riht hand, once.

Figure: 9

Wipe the inner sides of the ears with the forefingers, and their outer sides with the thumbs.

Figure: 10

Wipe around the neck with the wet back of the rest of the fingers.

Figure: 11

Wash the right foot up to the ankles. Beginning from the toes.

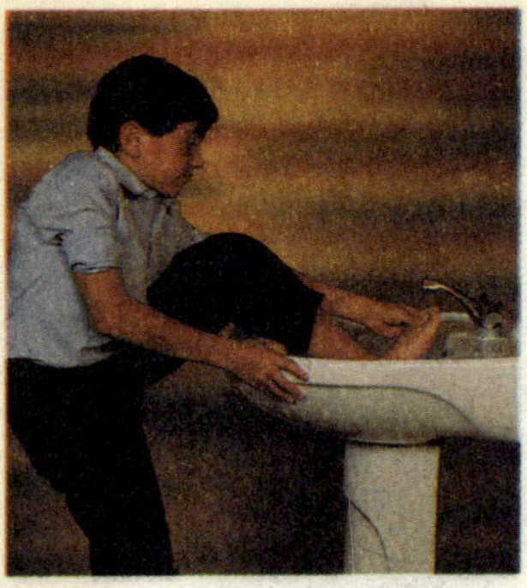

Figure: 12

Wash the left foot up to the ankles. Make sure that the parts between the toes is cleaned.

THE COMPLETE ABLUTION (GHUSL/BATH)

One who is in the ritual impurity *(junûb)* can only become clean from this state *(janâbat)* again by *ghusl.*

It becomes fard to wash the whole body with the nostrils, mouth and head by a complete bath in any of the following cases:

1- The state of Janâbat **occurs by;**

a- an intimate intercourse,

b- wet dreams.

c- effusion of semen ***(maniy)*** caused by sensual reasons.

2- Upon expiration of the menstruation period of women ***(hayd)***.

3- At the end of the confinement period (puerperium) of nursing woman ***(nıfas)***, which is estimated of fourty days. If it ends before, the *ghusl* should be taken then.

The *Fards* of the *Ghusl:*

1- Taking water into the mouth and gargling, three times.

2- Sniffing up water to the nostrils

3- Washing the whole body without leaving even a pin point dry spot (including the navel).

The *Sunnats* of the *Ghusl*:

1- Declaration of the intention

2- Saying the 'Audhu-Basmala'

3- Cleansing the body from the remnant dirt

4- Washing the privy parts

5- Taking *wudû'*

6- Pouring water over the head, after that, over the right shoulder, then over the left shoulder.

7- Rubbing the body while washing.

8- Washing the feet if they remain in the puddle of used *ghusl* water.

HOW THE *GHUSL* İS TAKEN

It should be pointed out at the start of the *ghusl*, the intention must be clear that it is for the purpose of purity and worship.

Pronouncing the ***aûdhu-basmala.***

Washing the hands up to the wrists.

Washing the privy parts.

Washing the hands again.

Taking normal *wudû'*.

Washing the whole body, three times.

It must be made sure that: ear-ring wholes, inner parts of the ears, bottom of hair and the navel, have been cleaned.

The *junûb* cannot legally perform:

a- valid *salât*

2- *tawâf* round the Ka'ba

c- staying in a mosque (except in cases of necessity)

d- touching the copies of the Qur'an

e- quoting verses (except for the supplication purpose)

THE *TAYAMMUM* (ABLUTION TAKEN WITH SAND)

Tayammum or resort to pure earth may substitute for the

ablution and even the bath. It is a symbolic demonstration of the importance of the ablution, which is so vital for both worship and health. When Islam introduced this repeatable ablution, it brought along with it the best hygienic formula which no other spiritual doctrine or medical prescription had anticipated.

Who are Eligible to Perform *Tayammum?*

1- When a person is sick and cannot use water.

2- When he has no access to water in sufficient quantity.

3- When the use of water is likely to do him harm or cause any disease, because of cold e.t.c.

4- When the performance of ablution makes the person miss a funeral or *Îd* prayer, which has no substitute.

In any of these instances it permissible to make *'Tayammum'*.

How the *Tayammum* is Performed?

1- Strike both hands slightly on pure earth or sand or stone.

2- Shake the hands off and wipe the face with them once in the same way as done in the ablution.

3- Strike the hands again and wipe the right arm to the elbow with the left hand and the left arm with the right hand.

The *Fards* of *Tayammum*

1- Declaration of the *wudû'* intention.

2- Wiping the hands and the face.

Expiry of *Tayammum*

1- When the sufficient water is accessable

2- When the obstacles to use water are over

3- When one or both of the *mast* is taken off before the expiry.

Special Facilities for Ablution

With regard to the ablution Islam has offered certain facilities.

Mash (Wiping)

The mash is allowed in the following cases.

1- When the ***Mast*** (light thin-soled boots) have been put on after performing an ablution.

They should not be put off and wash the feet whenever an ablution is to be performed. Instead of taking them off, the wet hand may be passed over them. They should be removed, however, and the feet washed at least once in every twenty-four hours. This duration can be extended up to three days for the traveller.

The *mast* must not be torn or unraveled, which are to be strong enough to resist for a six kilometer-walk. They are also to be made of watertight materials.

2- If there is a wound in any of the parts which must be washed in the *ghusl* and *wudû*, and if washing is likely to cause harm or worsenes it, then it is permissible to wipe the dressing bandage of the wound with a wet hand.

Reneval of the dressing does not necessarily requires anew mash.

SECTION FOUR

THE FASTING *(SAWM)*

Another unique moral and spiritual characteristics of Islam is the institution of Fasting. Literally defined, fasting means; to abstain completely from foods, drinks, intimate intercourses and smoking, before the break of the dawn till sunset, during the entire month of Ramadan.

Ramadan is a month in which the Kur'an started to be revealed. In it there is the 'Night of Power' ***(Laylat al-Qadr)*** which is dearer than a thousand months.

The meaning of the Fasting is wider since it has personal and social benefits.

The Benefits of the Fasting

1- It teaches man the principle of sincere Love; because when he observes the Fasting he does it out of deep love for God. And the man who loves God truly is a man who really knows what love is.

2- It equips man with a creative sense of Hope and an optimistic outlook on life; because when he fasts he is hoping to please God and is seeking His Grace.

3- It imbues man with a genuine virtue of effective. Devotion, honest Dedication and closeness to God; because when he fasts he does so for God and for His sake alone.

4- It cultivates in man a vigilant and sound Conscience; because the fasting person keeps his Fast in secret as well as in public. In Fasting, especially, there is no mundane authority to check man's behaviour or compel him to observe the Fasting. He keeps it to please God any satisfy his own conscience by being faithful in secret and in public. There is no better way to cultivate a sound conscience in man.

5- It indoctrinates man in Patience and Unselfishness;

because when he fasts he feels the pains of deprivation but endures patiently. Truly this deprivation may be only temporary, yet there is no doubt that the experience makes him realize the severe effects of such pains on others, who might be deprived of essential commodities for days and weeks or probably months together. The meaning of this experience in a social and humanitarian sense is that such a person is much quicker than anybody else in sympathizing with his fellow men and responding to their needs.

6- It is an effective lesson im applied Moderation and Willpover. The Fasting person can dscipline his passionate desires and place his physical temptation. This provides him a strong character and determination. When he fasts he is in control of himself, exercises full command over himself.

7- It enables man to master the art of Mature adaptability.

8- It originates in man the real Spirit of Social Belonging, of Unity and Brotherhood, of Equality before God as well as before the Law.

Who is bound to Fast?

The Fasting of Ramadan is compalsory upon every Muslim, male or female who has these qualifications:

1- To be mentally and physically fit, which means to be sane and abl.

2- To be of full age, the age of puberty and discretion. Children under this age should be encouraged to start this practice on easy levels.

3- To be present at the permanet settlement, the home town ***(muqîm)***. This means not to be travelling on a journey of about ninety kilometers or more ***(musâfir)***.

4- To be fairly certain that the Fasting is unlikely to cause any harm, physical or mental, other than the normal reactions to hunger, thirst, etc.

Exemption From Fasting

1- Sickness:

Sick people whose health is likely to be severely affected by the observance of fasting. They may postpone the fast, as long as they are sick, to a later date and make up for it, a day for a day.

2- Travel:

People in the course of travelling of distances about ninety kilometers or more. In this case such people may break the fast temporarily during their travel only and make up for it in later days, a day for a day. But it is better for them to keep the fasting if they can, without causing hardships.

3- Expectant and nursing woman:

She may break the fast, if its observance is likely to endanger their own health or that of their infant. But they must make up for the fast at a delayed time, a day for a day.

4- Menstrutaion and puerperium:

Woman in the period of menstruaiton and puerperium, is not allowed to fast even if they can and want to. They must pustpone the fast till recovery and then make up for it, a day for a day.

5- Elderliness and Feebleness:

Too old and feeble persons are exempted from the fast, but they must offer, at least, one needy poor Muslim an average full meal or its value per person per day. This is terminologically celled compensation ***(Fidya)***. Those who have incurable disease and cannot fast, if financially possible, should pay *fidya* in the same way.

The *Niyat*:

As in other Islamic undertakings, the intention must be made clear that the fast is undertaken for the sake of God and in His obedience. Without niyat the fast is invalid.

When to Make the *Niyat*:

It can be done after the break of the fast in the evening ***(ıftâr)*** till the forenoon of the next day. But normally it should be made after the meal *(sahûr)*. It is not obligatory to have *sahûr*. The niyat is done by heart suffices.

The niyat for the redemption *(kaffarat)* and the fastings out of the Ramadan is done at night, not after the break of the dawn *(ımsâk)*.

The Things Make the Fast Void *(muftırât)*

The fast of any day of Ramadan becomes void by:

1- Intentional eating or drinking or smoking.

2- Indulgence in any intimate intercources.

3- Mestruation

4- Allowing anything to enter through the mouth in the interior part of the body. And if this is done deliberately without any lawful reason, the penalty is to observe the fast of sixty consecutive days or, as a second alternative if physically is not fit, to feed sixty poor persons sufficiently.

5- Deliberate seminal emission. Nocturnal or similar emission ***(ihtilâm)*** is not *muftîr.*

6- Deliberate vomiting, which is only permitted by doctor's order and even then only with liability to make up.

If anyone, by mistake, does something that would ordinarily break the fast, his observance is not nullified, and his fast stands valid, provided he stops doing that thing at the moment he realizes what he is doing.

The Categories of the Fast

1- *Fard* (Imperative) Fasts

The Fasting of Ramadan, and the day for a day fastings *(Qadâ)*. The atonment *(kaffarat)* Fastings.

2- *Wajib* Fasts:

Vowed Fastings, the *qadâ* of the broken supererogatory *(nafl)* Fastings.

3- *Sunnat* Fasts:

The two day Fasting on the ninth, and tenh or the tenth and eleventh days of the month Muharram.

4- *Mustahab* Fasts:

The thirteenth, fourteenth and fifteenth days of every lunar month. Mondays and Thursdays of every week. Six days after the Ramadan in the Shawwal month.

5- *Makrûh* Fasts:

Only on the tenth day of the Muharram. Only on the Fridays and only the Saturdays.

6- *Haram Fasts:*

The first day of the *'Îd al-Fıtr,* and four days of the *'Îd al-Adhâ*. For a woman during menstruation.

THE OATH *(YAMÎN)*

Breaking an earnest oath results to expiation.

The Categories of the Oath:

1- Yamin *laghw* (The Null Oath):

It is lie oath made by mistake. No expiation is required.

2- Yamin *Ghamûs* (The Ominous Oath):

It is a lie oath which is intentionally done. For example; though he has not seen something he oathes that he has seen it. Such action is a grave sin. Allah only can forgive him provided he demanded forgiveness.

2- Yamîn *Mun'aqada* (The conttracted Oath):

It is an oath made for a future action. Breaking such oath results to expiation for the offender. For example; I swear by God that I will do such thing tomorrow. If it is not done it means breaking the oath. In this case;

the offender:

a- Feeds or clothes ten indigent persons, if this is not possible,

b- Emancipates a slave or ransom his freedom. If that is not possible,

c- Fasts of three days in sequence as the last resort.

SECTION FIVE

ZAKÂT (THE ALMS)

Another major pillar of Islam is the *zakât*. It is an exceptionally remarkable institution. Literally it means 'purity'. Technically designates the annual amount in kind or in coin which a Muslim must distribute among the rightful beneficiaries. It is not just a form o charity or alms-giving or alms-giving or tax of tithe. Nor is it simply an expression of kindness; it is all of these combined and much more. The religious and spiritual signifigance of it is much deeper.

Rather, it is a duty enjoined by God and undertaken by Muslims in interest of society as a whole. It is a sipiritual investment. It contains spiritual and moral motives. So it is a humanitarian and sociopolitical value. *Zakât* purifies the property and clears it from the shares which do not belong to it anymore. The owner no longer has moral or legal possession of the percentage to be distributed as *Zakât*. If he fails to do so, he is obviously retaining something which does not belong to him. This is corruption and plain usurpation from every point of view, moral and sipiritual, legal and commercial.

Zakât does not only purify the property of the contributor but also purify his heart from selfishness; and it fosters in his heart, instead, good will and warm wishes.

Zakât is a healthy from of internal security against greed and social dissensions. It is an effective instrument in cultivating the spirit of social responsibility on the part of the contributor, and the feeling of security and belonging on the part of the recipient.

Who Pays *Zakât?*

Every Muslim, male or female, who is rich according to Islamic criterion ***(nısâb)***.

Who is Rich?

The person who, after the main necessities; a house, households and a car etc, owns the amount of the nisâb and keeps it a period of a lunar year.

What is *Nisâb?*

It is an amount of 80.18 gr. gold or its equivalent in money.

What kind of Wealth is Subject to *Zakât?*

Productive property, namely; gold, silver, cattle, articles of trade in the stores, and agricultural products.

When a person has wealth in business stocks or trade articles, he must evaluate his wealth at the end of the year according to the current value and give *zakât*.

If this investment is immovable property like revenue buildings and industries, the *zakât* should go by the total net of the income, not of the total value of the whole property, provided the revenue kept for a year. But if it was invested then no *zakât* is due.

If someone puts up buildings and houses for trade or selling, *zakât* should go by the total value of the entire property.

If someone is a creditor and the indebted person is reliable one should pay the *zakât* for the amount he has lent because it is still a portion of his guaranteed wealth.

What is the Rate of *Zakât?*

It is 2.5% out of the property other than the cattle and agriculturel products. The shares payable in these regard vary, and needed a detailed discussion. So the reader may be advised to consult the elaborate sources of Law and religion.

Is *Niyat* required?

Niyat is essential also in the *Zakât*. But the *zakât* payer should not seek pride or fame by caryying out this duty. He should make it as covert as possible. So as not to humilate the recipient he may not declare that it is a *zakât*. The *niyat* by heart is sufficient.

The Recipients of Zakât

1- The needy and the poor (***faqîr*** and ***miskîn***)

They are the ones who has nothing to meet their basic necessities.

2- The Muslim in debt.

3- The *zakât* collectors.

4- The Muslim wayfarers.

5- The Muslim in service of the cause of God; by means of research or study etc.

6- The new Muslim converts.

7- Soldiers.

8- war prisionars.

Zakât may be distributed directly to individuals of one or more of the said classe, or the welfare organizations which look after them. It may also be distributed in the form of scholarships.

The disabled or invalid poor is preferable to one who is able and capable of making some earnings.

Persons and Purposes Who may not be Zakat Beneficiaries

1- The *zakât* payer's ascending and descending relatives, i.e, parents, sons and grand sons etc.

2- Husband and wife.

3- The rich person.

4- The persons in the linage of the Prophet Muhammad ***(Banû Hâshîm)***.

5- mosques, schools etc.

6- Non-Muslim.

SADAQAT AL-FITR

On completion of the fast of Ramadan, the special charity known as ***sadaqat-al-fıtr*** (Charity of Fast-beraking) must be distributed.

It is paid by the persons who are rich as described above. It should be paid 1460 grams of wheat, or 2920 grams of barley, or dry grapes. Or their equivalent in money.

Rich parents also should pay for their children.

It is subject to *zakât* system in other matters.

It is a *wâjib* charity.

It is recommended to be distributed before the *'Îd Prayer* has been performed.

SECTION SIX

THE PILGRIMAGE (HAJI)

The final pillar of Islam is the *Haji* or pilgrimage to Mecca.

It is the largest annual convention of Faith where Muslims meet te know one another, and promote their general welfare. It is the greatest regular conference of peace known in the history of mankind.

In the course of *Hajj* peace is the dominant theme; peace with God and one's soul, peace with one another and with animals, peace with birds and even with insects. To disturb the peace of anyone or any creatures in any shape or form results to a penalty, such as sacrifising an animal.

It is a wholesome demonstration of the universality of Islam and the brotherhood and equality of the Muslims. From all trades and classe, and from every corner of the globe the Muslims assemble at Mecca in response to the call of God. There, there is no aristocracy, but humiliation and devotion. There is no royalty but loyalty of all to God.

It is to commemorate the divine rituals observed by Abraham and Ishmael, who are known to have been the first pilgrims to the first house of God an earth, i.e., the Ka'ba at Mecca.

It is a symbolic assembly of the Grand Assembly on the Day of Judgement when people will stand equal before God, waiting for their Final Destiny.

The description of the rules and steps followed during the *Hajj* are rather lengthy. They will not be discussed here.

Who is Obliged to Make *Hajj?*

Every Muslim, male or female, who is of responsible age, mentally, financially and physically fit.

The Muslim contains these conditions must make the *Hajj* once in his or her lifetime.

The financial security here means that he could have enough to cover his own expenses and those of his dependents, and to pay his debts, if he is indebted.

To make *Hajj* is an imperative *(fard)* duty.

What are the Fard rites *(manâsik)* of the *Hajj*?

1- Wearing ***Ihrâm*** (garb worm by the pilgrim at ***Mîqât)***

2- Paying visit and making ***Tawâf*** (sevenfold circumambulation) to Ka'ba.

3- ***Wakfa*** (making a halt) in the plains of Mount ***'Arafât***

What are the *Wâjibs* of the *Hajj*?

1- To be peresent ***(wukûf)*** in the Muzdalifa on the first day of *'Id al-Adhâ* between the dawn and sunrise.

2- Iapidation at the symbolic Satans before having the hair cut.

3- Sacrificing an animal by the pilgrims who are making the *Qırân* and *Tamattu 'Hajj*.

4- Having the hair cut and being shaved.

5- To make ***Sa'y*** *(sevenfold fast walking* ***(harwala)*** between the Safâ and Marwa Hills neighbouring the Ka'ba). This should be performed on the pilgrimage days and after *Tawâf*.

6- Beginning to the ***Sa'y*** from the Safâ hill.

7- To perform the farewell *Tawâf* ***(Tawaf Wadâ)***, for those pilgrims coming from abroad.

8- To perform *Tawâf* in the state of ablution.

9- To pray two *rak'ats* at the end of *Tawâf*.

10- To perform the last three *Shawt* (each turning around the Ka'ba) of visiting *Tawâf* at the arrival ***(Tawaf Qudûm)***

What are the Types of *Hajj?*

1- Qırân (combination):

Performance of the pilgrimage and *'umra* with one *ihrâm*. The niyat made when the *ihrâm* is put on should cover both the *'umra* and the *hajj*. In this type of *Hajj* sacrifice is a *wâjib*. On the arrival in Mecca; first the *'umra* then the *tawâf qudûm* and the sa'y of the *hajj* are to be performed.

2- *Tamattu* (enjoyment):

Performance of the 'umra and hajj in seperate ihrâms. That is; first, performing the *'umra,* and taking off the *ihrâm*. When the day before Eve ***(yawm tarwiya)*** comes wearing the *ihrâm* again for the performance of the Hajj. Also in this *Hajj* sacrifice is *wâjib*.

3- *Ifrâd* (seperation):

In this *hajj* there is no *'umra,* only the *Hajj* is performed. No sacrifice is required.

The Procedure of the *Hajj*

In the vicinity of Mecca three are places called *Mîqât* where the pilgrims put on the pilgrims put on the *ihrâms* (sacred ware). One who is in this state is called *muhrim*. This garment consists of two seamless wrappers. One is called ***izâr*** which to be wrapped around the waist. The other is ***ridâ*** which is to be thrown over the shoulders. Here, two *rak'at-sunnat* prayer is performed.

Mîqât:

There are several stations ***(mawâqît,*** plur. of ***mîqât)*** where the *ihrâm* is usually put on namely: ***Dhul Hulayfa,*** for the pilgrims from al-Madîna. ***Al-Juhfa,*** for those from Syria and Egypt. ***Qarn al-Manâzil,*** for those from Najd. ***Yalamlam,*** for those from Yaman. ***Dhât 'Irq,*** for those from 'Iraq.

Anyone who assumes *ihrâm* too late has later to sacrifice an animal in atonement.

The people who live within the area shall assume the *ihrâm* in their dwellings, when it is a question of performing the *hajj.* For an 'umra they must go to one of the boundary places of the *hill* (the area outside the *Harâm*); usually Tan'îm is chosen for this purpose.

Then the intention must be declared for *hajj.* It should be accompanied with the pray called *Talbiyat,* or *Labbayk* which is:

لبيك اللهم لبيك لبيك لاشريك لك لبيك

ان الحمد و النعمة لك والملك لاشريك لك

"Labbayk Allahumma labbayk. Labbayka la sharika laka labbayk. Innalhamda wanni'mata laka walmulk. La sharika lak".

This is continually pronounced during the *hajj* up to the lapidation *(jamrât).* On the arrival in Mecca a *wudû'* is taken. Then going to Ka'ba and a *tawâf ziyârat* is made. The Black Stone ***(Hajar Aswad)*** is greeted. A two *rak'at* prayer follows it. Subsequently, ***Sa'y*** is made.

On the ***Tarwiya day*** (the day before the Eve of *Îd* of *Adhâ*) moving to Mount 'Arafat and staying there until the sunset. Then moving to Muzdalifa and performing *Maghrib* Prayer and *'Îshâ* Prayer are performed combinedly ***(Jam')*** in the latter's time there. And collect the shingels for stoning the Satans.

In the morning of the first day of the *'Îd*; perform the ***Fajr*** Prayer early and after, make ***wakfa*** there.

On the first day of the *'Îd*; stoning the Great Satan *(Jamrat 'Aqabat)* is done, the *ifrad* hajj makers have their hair cut. The *qırân* and the *tamattu'* hajj makers after the sacrifice has been slaughtered have their hair cut. Then the ihrâms is removed. If there is time, going to Mecca and making the *tavâf* ziyârat.

On the second day of the *'Îd*; Small, Medium and the Great Satans are stonned with seven shingels to each. Those who missed the *Tawâf Ziyârat* which is a *fard*, can make it on this day.

On the third day; The same satans in the same order are stonned with seven shingels to each.

The same day, the *Tawâf* wadâ is performed. Now, the *Hajj* is completed any moving to Madina follows.

In Madina, The Tomb of the Holy Prophet ***(Masjid Nabawî)*** is visited. It is not an essential obligation in making the *Hajj* valid and complete. But it is always advisable and strongly recommended that whoever can reach to Madina should visit and pay respect to the greatest teacher that humanity has ever known.

'UMRA (THE LITTLE PILGRIMAGE)

In any time, wearing ihrâm, making Tawaf, Sa'y, and shaving constitute the 'umra. It is a sunnat.

It can be made in any time of the year except on the Eve and the *'Îd Adhâ* days.

The Performance of the 'Umra

On assuming the *ihrâm* the ***mu'tamir*** (*'umra* maker) must make up his mind whether he is going to perform the *'umra* by itself or in combination with the *hajj* and express his intention in an appropriate *niyat*. If he combines the *'umra* with *hajj* he can assume the *ihrâm* for both. In the other case the *ihrâm* must be specially assumed for the *'umra* in the unconsecrated area ***(Hill)*** outside *harâm* of Mecca. This holds also for native Meccans who, when they are going to perform the *hajj* can assume the *ihrâm* within Mecca.

With the utterance of ***labbayk*** the actual ceremony of

'umra begins and also of the *hajj*. The *mu'tamir* goes to Mecca in order, first of all to go around the Ka'ba *(tawâf)*. He enters the mosque through the north door of the northeast side *(Bab al- Salâm)*, goes under the portal of the *Banû Shayba* to the Black Stone built into the wall of the Ka'ba and turning right, begins the sevenfold *tawâf* of the Ka'ba, saying prays all the while. The first three *shawt* are performed at a rapid pace *(ramal)*, the four last an ordinary rate. After this is finished.

In conclusion he performes two *rak'ats* behind the *Makâm Ibrâhîm*, drinks af draught of the holy *Zemzem* water. The *mu'tamir* now leaves the mosque through the great *al-Safa* door in order to perform the second essential part of the *'umra*, the sa'y. He has thus completed the ceremony of the *'umra*, and has only to have his hair cut or be shaved. If he is making the *'umra*, in combination with the *hajj*, he only has his hair trimmed and has the proper cutting done on the 10th of *Zul Hijja* at the end of the *hajj*.

SECTION SEVEN

SACRIFICE

It is a wâjib obligation for whose wealth amounts to *nisâb* after meeting the basic necesseties.

Sacrifice is slaughtering an animal worth sacrificing within the days of the *'Îd Adhâ* with the intention of worship. It is not the meat or blood that pleases God. It is an expression of thankfulness to Him, and an affirmation of faith in Him.

It is an annual celebration to commemorate Abraham and his son Ishmael. Prophet Abraham was ordered to offer his son in sacrifice, an order which the father and son were ready to obey unquestioningly, But the son's life was spared and ransomed by a ram.

Animals worth sacrificing are;

Sheep, goats, cows, oxen and camels.

Sheep and goat are sacrificed by one person only. Cows, oxen, and camel may be sacrificed by up to seven persons.

The animals subject to sacrifice must be in good health, strong and free from disease and defects.

The meat of the sacrifice may be distributed to the poor or if needed, to be retained all of it for the person himself. But it is advisable to be divided into three parts; the first part goes to the poor, the second part to the friends and relatives, and the third part for the home use.

The sacrifice animals cannot be donated alive, because the slaughtering is essential. Donation is not a substitution. Their skin cannot be sold and may be donated to the poor or to charitable foundations.

SACRIFICE OF VOW *(NADHR)*

Vowe is an earnest pledge or promise binding the person making it to perform.

The vow is of two kinds

1- Unconditional vow:

This vow is made by saying: For the sake of God I will sacrifice an animal. Thereof, it becomes incumbent to act accordingly. There is no time limit fulfilling the obligation.

2- Conditional vow:

It is the kind of vow made for an occation subject to a condition. For example; if my illness gets cured I will sacrifice an animal for God's sake. It becomes an obligation to sacrifice an animal if his illness is heeled.

The sacrificial animals for a valid vow are the ones slaughtered for the *'Îd Adhâ.*

The meat of such sacrifice is not allowed to be consumed by the vower, and his or her ascendants and descendants. It must be distributed amongst the poor.

SACRIFICE FOR A DEAD PERSON

The sacrifice for a dead person should be slaughtered during the *'Îd Adhâ* days. The meat of such sacrifice can be consumed by the sacrificer.

The sacrifice slaughtered on the bequest of the deceased person the sacrificer cannot consume the meat. It should be distributed to the poor.

'AQÎQA

It is the name of the sacrifice on the seventh day after the birth of a child. It is recommendable ***(mustahab)***. On that day to give a name to the new-born child, to shave off its hair and to slaughter a sacrifice, for a boy; two rams or two he-goats, for girl; one of these suffices. If the offering of the *'aqîqa* has been neglected on the seventh day, it can be done afterwards, even by the child itself when it has come of age. The greater part of the flesh of the sacrifice is distributed amongst the poor and the indigent.

The shorn hair of the child is also called *'aqîqa,* not less than the weight of the hair, in silver or in gold as alms giving is to be spent.

CW01665583

Stories on the Go

Sandra Turner

Michael Terence Publishing

First published in paperback by
Michael Terence Publishing in 2018
www.mtp.agency

ISBN 9781912639090

This book is dedicated to…

My dad, for his inspiration

Noreen Ellisdon, who has been there since the beginning

Sonia Ribeiro, for believing in me

Peter Sartori, for his love & support

To Helen
Best Wishes
Sandra Turner
18/6/22

11 Stories on the Go

Sandra Turner

CONTENTS

HARRIETT ROWBOTHAM

The perfect partner for Harriet Rowbotham was Paul Dobson. The trouble was he had not yet realised this. She felt certain he would reach this conclusion too and would not allow any doubts to surface in her mind. Why.... had he not readily come to her assistance on Saturday when she had locked herself out of her house? Insisted even that she get down from the ladder and let him climb in through the open bathroom window?. Afterwards, she had invited him to stop awhile for coffee and homemade fruit-cake and he had told her how delicious it was, declaring 'You can always tell a home-made cake from a shop bought one, it tastes richer and far less sweet'. She had enquired then about Stephanie. Stephanie, the thorn in her side and her only obstacle in the way of getting closer to Paul. She really only asked because she thought it the polite thing to do. 'Does Stephanie do much baking?' Paul laughed as he answered 'Stephanie can't cook beans on toast without burning them. So I'd hate to see what she'd do to a cake!' Harriet was horrified but not surprised. A wry smile spread across her face as she realised that life with Stephanie must be hell on earth, eating pizzas and other takeaways that she had seen being delivered many times a week. Oh yes. Paul must be a patient and caring man. She loved him even more for this. But even his patience must surely wear thin over time? 'Won't you stay for another slice of cake?'

Harriet asked. 'Thanks but I really should be going. Steph will be home from work soon and there are still dirty dishes to be stacked in the dishwasher'. Harriet smiled, hoping that he wouldn't see the effort she had trying to keep the anger from her eyes. She wouldn't mind, but Stephanie didn't have a REAL job. Just filed and painted the nails of other empty air-heads like herself. But Harriet had to keep up the pretence. She knew it would take a while longer for Paul to seize the bait she would so lovingly prepare for him. 'I'll just see you to the door' 'There's no need' Paul said smiling 'I can find my own way out' then added 'perhaps I'll bring Stephanie over for a cup of tea one day so that the two of you can become better acquainted, What do you think?' 'How nice. I'll be sure to save some cake for her to try' 'Oh heavens, don't do that. Steph's permanently on a diet!' She had guessed as much. Steph was stick-thin and her face was sallow. Probably from lack of certain vitamins. Whilst her own figure was 'curvy'. Surely, Harriet thought, any man would prefer to grab at flesh than bone? She heard the click of the front door as Paul left and hurried quickly to the window-seat in time to see Paul; open his own front door and disappear inside.

About twenty minutes later, Harriet heard the familiar purr of Stephanie's sports car as it came up the drive. A pause, then the car door slammed, followed by Stephanie's voice as she called out 'Are you home babe? Can you give me a hand with my shopping? Harriet twitched the curtain as she looked out. No sign of food, only the reds and fluorescent pinks of clothes could be seen through the white plastic bags with the name 'Zaza's' emblazoned on the side. 'Only a harlot would wear such colours!' Harriet said to herself, as she smoothed down her brown. tweed, calf-length skirt. Stephanie's black skirt was so short it barely covered her bottom and her white stiletto shoes had at least a four-inch heel, Harriet guessed. Harriet thought of her father and how furious he would have been if she had ever dared to dress like this. 'Men don't marry tarts!' He'd boom at her often enough. But he'd changed his own rule when he ran off at aged sixty-four with his twenty-eight-year-old secretary. Leaving Harriet and her mother with nothing but the house and a pile of debts.

The front door opened and Stephanie disappeared inside empty-handed, leaving Paul to bring in all the bags from Zaza's. As Harriet watched Paul enter the house, a fresh wave of longing swept over her. If only Stephanie were to have an accident, Harriet thought. A little accident mind you, nothing life-threatening, just enough to keep her out of the way, Paul would naturally turn to Harriet for comfort, and she would give him such sweet comfort!

Harriet sat down at the kitchen table and set to work peeling and chopping apples. Her own apples from the garden. She would make an apple pie for tea. She pictured Paul at the other end of the table, tucking into good food for a change. He would say to her 'Oh Harriet, you certainly know the way to a man's heart, my heart. You spoil me too much' and she would reply 'I could never spoil you enough, my darling'. As Harriet sat there, head in hands, daydreaming, she wondered if she could invite Paul and Stephanie to tea. She could make an individual apple pie for each of them, she would slip a few seed-heads of henbane into Stephanie's pie. She would make sure each pie had an initial made of pastry on top. That way she could ensure that neither Paul or her would eat the pie containing Henbane! But this was foolish! Even if she could get Stephanie to eat the pie, and remembering the conversation she had with Paul earlier, doubted this to be so, the hospital would find Henbane in Stephanie's blood after tests and questions would be raised as to how she could have ingested this. No, this would not do, she scolded herself, she would have to think of something else.

******

When Harriet was a little girl she truly loved her father and he doted on his only daughter. Sunday was her favourite day, her father did not have to leave early to catch the train for work. They would do things together as a family. In the summer her mother would prepare fried chicken and potato salad, with apple pie or fairy cakes for dessert. This she would lovingly pack into a square, wicker basket and they would all pile into her father's motorcycle and sidecar and drive out into the countryside for a picnic, Harriet seated in the sidecar on her mother's lap. Well, it was the 1950s, and her father couldn't quite afford to buy a car, but Harriet loved to ride in the sidecar. Her father would be dressed from head to toe in black leather. How handsome he looked, she recalled. Much later, in 1968, when Harriet was fourteen and her father had been promoted, he came home one day with a white Triumph Herald convertible, which had a black soft-top roof. The motorcycle was banished to an old barn. It was around this time he started to change. Not at first, but soon afterwards. Harriet and her mother blamed that damn car! That first evening they all set off for a long ride, 'To run it in', her father had said. But thereafter he'd scream at Harriet to 'take off your muddy shoes!' or 'don't slam the car door!'. He no longer spent much time with her or her mother. Much of Sundays was spent cleaning and polishing the car. He came home later at night and explained that he had a lot more responsibilities at work since his promotion. So Harriet and her father drifted apart, never to regain that precious bond she'd shared with him as a child. She spent more and more time with her mother who taught her how to cook and sew, for which she was now grateful as she made all her own clothes. None of the shop-bought garments, and as for Madam Zaza's, Harriet swore she would never set foot inside the door. One good thing Harriet's father had taught her at age twelve was how to strip down the motorcycle, clean and oil the parts and put it all back together again.

Harriet loved the motorcycle and sidecar and had kept it all these years. As far as she knew it was in good working order. Maybe it was time for Harriet to take it out on a test run. Harriet smiled to herself, a plan half-forming in her mind.

The very next day, Harriet allowed herself one boiled egg only for breakfast and one slice of toast, she wanted to be at her best for the task ahead and not sluggish from eating a heavy meal. She ran a shallow bath, refusing to have the bathroom modernised with a new electric shower. She loved to indulge herself in a long leisurely soak in fragrant-smelling bath salts. The only 'shower' she allowed herself was an attachment to the bath taps so she could wash and rinse her hair properly. She stepped out of the bath and dried herself in a now yellowing fluffy bath towel that she had bought herself years ago from John Lewis when she had visited a sick aunt in London. The towel, although old, was still luxuriously soft and fluffy. So it should be, she thought. It had cost a pretty penny!. She wandered into the bedroom still swathed in the towel, she bent to retrieve an old, battered suitcase from beneath the bed and as she stood up the towel slipped to the floor. She stood naked and looked at herself in the full-length mirror and was pleased with what she saw. Although not large, her bosoms were round and full, And my own! She thought. Her stomach although also round, was not fat. Her thighs were full although slightly dimpled with cellulite, but that was natural for a woman of her age, wasn't it? Her legs were thickset but still had a good shape to them. She now recalled that at sixteen she had been on a holiday to Butlins at Clacton-on-Sea with her mother and aunt and had won £5.00 in a 'Miss Lovely Legs' competition. She turned towards her bed, her one extravagance. It was a double-bed with interior-sprung mattress, she couldn't abide single beds, no room to stretch out in, and in her mind's eye could see Paul staring at her body appreciatively! 'Oh Harriet', he would say, 'What a fool I have been waiting so long for this moment!' She would run to him and they would make love all night long, just like in her romantic novels she fetched from the library in town each week. Her mind snapped back to the present. She retrieved a pair of old dungarees from the suitcase and dressed quickly in these, together with a paint-stained but clean brushed-cotton check shirt. She hurried to the kitchen and put on a pair of Wellington boots then ran out to the small barn where the motorcycle was housed and wheeled it into the yard.

Firstly, a bucket of warm, soapy water was required. To wash away the years of built up cobwebs and dirt. This Harriet brought from the kitchen with a sponge and long-handled brush to clean in between the tyres and spokes of the wheels. It was hard work, and Harriet paused after a while, wondering if she was doing the right thing. Then she thought of Paul and how Stephanie took him for granted and she returned to her task with renewed vigour.

It may have been because she was so focused on her task, or because she was listening to Mozart on her personal CD player, that she didn't hear the footsteps behind her. The quick tap on her shoulder made her jump, and she gave out a little cry of alarm. It was Paul 'Sorry Harriet, I didn't mean to startle you. I did call out to you but you were so engrossed in what you were doing, you mustn't have heard me'. 'My, oh my' Harriet replied taking off the headphones, 'what a frightful mess I must look!' 'Well, you are hardly going to wear your best clothes for the job in hand are you now?' Paul said, flashing a smile at Harriet. Such wonderful white teeth, Harriet thought, and his blue eyes crinkle at the corners when he smiles. 'Where on earth did you get such a wonderful old motorcycle?' Harriet was extremely pleased with Paul's enquiry. 'It belonged to my father' she said, 'It's a 648cc Panther, built in a place called Cleckheaton in Yorkshire. They were quite popular in the 1950s'

'Is it in good working order' Paul enquired

'I'll find that out just as soon as I've serviced the engine'

'Why Harriet, you are a dark horse. You'll be telling me next that you have a fetish for leather and listen to Heavy Metal'

'What's that?' Harriet enquired.

Never mind' Paul laughed, 'It was just a joke. I'm off into town to pick up Steph. Her car is in the garage for a minor repair and a scratch to the bumper. But I'm fascinated by this old motorcycle. 1950s you say? It must be a collector's item. You'll let me know if you get it working? I'd love to take it for a spin'.

Harriet was overjoyed! What was that old saying? Something about your life coming round in full circle? She could look forward to summers again in the countryside, but this time it would be Paul by her side and not her father. They would go on picnics together. Spend days at the seaside and watch the sun go down together. All this was so possible, Harriet could feel it. There was one small problem, and it needed to be dealt with swiftly.

Her work done, Harriet decided it was time to take the motorcycle for a run. She took off her clothes, which were now oily and dirty. What sort of clothing do I have that is suitable to wear on a motorcycle? she asked herself. She looked through her clothes in the wardrobe and decided upon the clothes she normally wore when out hill walking, a pair of brown corduroy trousers, a beige cable-knit jumper, thick blue socks and chocolate-brown leather walking boots. She would need something to wear on her head. She thought of something, if only she could remember where she had stored it. Maybe it was in the trunk in the basement, together with a few other personal things she had kept which had belonged to her parents.

She went to the kitchen, put her hand on the door which led down into the basement and shuddered. She was not afraid of spiders, they kept the place clean in their own way, trapping flies and bluebottles in their silken webs, spinning cocoons over their prey so they could not escape and leaving them to devour at a later time when hungry. No, Harriet's thoughts turned to mice......or even rats, heaven forbid! as she turned on the cellar light and fancied she saw a shape scuttling around at the foot of the stairs where the light didn't quite reach and she shrieked in alarm. Pull yourself together, she scolded, but she fetched the broom with her, just in case, as she descended the stairs.

At the foot of the stairs, Harriet flicked a switch and with a buzz, buzz, pop the basement was flooded in light. No mice, no rats, whatever she'd seen, or thought she had seen had probably fled at the first sign of this intruder into their usually undisturbed world. In a far corner, underneath an old table and faded velvet curtains, Harriet retrieved a wooden chest. She placed a silver key into the lock and with little effort, the key turned. She lifted the lid and gazed upon all kinds of memorabilia from her childhood. Gently she lifted out an old Oxo tin, which was full of old black and white photographs of her and her parents. She put this to one side. Her eyes fell upon a book entitled 'Biggles Learns to Fly'. She remembered her father reading the story to her, and later 'Biggles in Africa', 'Biggles Goes to War' and Biggles - Secret Agent'. She couldn't get enough of these stories as a child. Her imagination would soar up into the clouds, along with Biggles and his exciting adventures, taking her to places she could only dream of. She also put these lovingly aside and found her prize, her father had given it to her one birthday, it had been a present from his father, a leather Biggles helmet, complete with goggles! Yes, this would serve her purpose well. She put everything back neatly in its place. Put the locked trunk back beneath the velvet curtains and left her memories behind as she ascended the basement steps.

Suitably attired, Harriet placed the key in the ignition and turned it. The red light blinked, then remained steady, the speedometer needle flew to the right and returned back to zero. These old motorcycles had a 'kick-start' lever, Harriet had watched her father perform this action whilst making a slight twist of the throttle, many times, this she repeated now. Nothing happened. She took a deep breath, said a silent prayer and tried again. A loud bang, followed by a cloud of black smoke from the exhaust, but the engine turned over and soon it was purring like a contented cat. Harriet breathed a sigh of relief, and climbed aboard the machine, pulling the goggles down over her eyes. Out of practice, the motorcycle wobbled in her hands a few times, but Harriet felt confident and was soon expertly riding towards town.

Harriet felt exhilarated. The speedometer climbed slowly, 15..... 20..... 25......30..... 35..... 40, it crept up to 60. The lampposts whizzed by in a blur. Harriet had not felt this excitement and freedom in years. She was hogging the centre of the road, and loving every minute. Suddenly from around the bend a delivery van appeared, its driver tooted the horn and shouted through the open window 'Pull over you stupid cow!'. Harriet expertly swerved to the left and laughed as she raised a two-finger salute to the driver. Was this how it felt to be intoxicated?..... in love? Whatever she felt, it seemed to envelop her very being.

On and on she rode, a sign ahead told Harriet she was approaching a roundabout, she reduced her speed but could see the road ahead had hardly any traffic so she took the roundabout and right exit at 40mph! Approaching her on the opposite side of the road, two motorcyclists rode, one behind the other. Harriet shouted a greeting of 'Hi, fellow riders'. One of the riders in turn shouted back, 'That's a wicked machine, sister' and he raised a fist in salute as he sped by.

She was fast approaching the town now and knew enough to reduce her speed to a cruising 30mph. The motorcycle shuddered, as if in protest to this sudden reduction in speed, but not long enough for Harriet to lose control. She slowed right down as the traffic lights ahead turned to red and pedestrians crossed as the green man 'beep-beeped' telling them it was safe to do so. A sign ahead caught Harriet's eye, it blazed at her in red 'Got it Nailed!', she only had time to read manicures and Acrylics from the list below as she rode by. Two women and a man stood outside on the pavement talking, Harriet recognised one of the females to be her arch-enemy, for this is how she viewed Stephanie. She had ridden by before she realised and would now have to stay on the road out of town as it was one-way, but she could ride in a circle and come back again. Harriet imagined the man had raised his hand to his forehead in a salute, as if he had recognised her. Her thoughts returned to Stephanie as the road took her full circle and she found herself once again on the outskirts of town.

Her emotions seemed to be heightened and her hatred of Stephanie overwhelmed her and quick as a flash, she knew what she had to do.

Harriet twisted the throttle a few times, the motorcycle vroom-vroomed and startled passers-by looked at her briefly and hurried along out of the way of this mad person. Harriet could see Stephanie clearly, everything else faded from sight.

She could see the short black skirt, the white stiletto heels, the white tunic top and her long blonde hair swept up into a French plait. The other female said something to Stephanie whose head tilted back and she shrieked with laughter. Harriet believed that they were laughing at her. Laughing at her plainness compared to their over-painted faces and over-coiffed hairstyles, their exaggerated fingernails painted red, resembling talons. With trembling hands, Harriet revved the motorcycle once more and the machine flew off with a life of its own. It zig-zagged across the road, barely missing a woman with a pushchair, the motorcycle mounted the pavement and Harriet closed her eyes, the last thing she remembered before hitting a lamp-post and falling into unconsciousness, was a blood-curdling scream.

******

Harriet awoke to mayhem. Two ambulances stood in the road nearby, their blue lights flashing. She had a thumping headache and paramedics had placed an oxygen mask over her face and were giving her CPR. 'My heart is working well' she managed to say to one of the young men tending her. 'This lady has regained consciousness' he shouted to a nearby policeman who turned and walked towards Harriet. 'Tell me', Harriet asked 'What happened to the woman I hit?' The policeman spoke to her 'You mean Ms Sinclair? She is unhurt save for a few scratches. Thanks to the quick reactions of her fiancée, Mr Dobson, she was pushed completely out of the way. Mr Dobson, however, was less fortunate. Your motorcycle slowed considerably when a wooden crate from the nearby fruit stall was caught beneath the wheels. Nontheless, Mr Dobson has sustained a broken leg, multiple fractures and is concussed' then his manner became more serious as he said to Harriet 'Ms Rowbotham, you will be charged with reckless and dangerous driving. You have the right to remain silent.....'

JUST DESSERTS

She stood outside the shop window fully appreciating the fine quality and craftsmanship. These were no ordinary boots. They were hand-made Italian leather, red in colour with a slim black heel, in perfect contrast.

Her heart beat fast, and she felt dizzy as she pushed open the heavy glass door and walked inside, but she was determined to do this.
“Can I help you madam?” a voice enquired.
'Yes, please. You have a pair of red Dolcini boots in the window, could I try them on? size four'.
'Certainly. I’ll just check to see if we have your size in stock'.
She felt the blush travel up her neck and into her cheeks. Could the shop assistant tell that she was a fake? She took in a deep breath to calm her nerves and exhaled slowly. The shop assistant was returning with a white box under his arm. 'These are the last pair in your size' he said, undoing the zip and passing them to her.
Slowly, she put her foot inside the boot, drawing the zip to the top and adjusting the side straps. She put on the second boot and walked up and down a few times, stopping at the mirror to admire her reflection. 'They are so comfortable' she said to the shop assistant.
'Madam’s legs are slim enough to compliment the boots' he said grinning. She wondered if this was a

sales pitch but felt her cheeks burning anyway. She walked up and down a few more times and then said. 'I'll take them please, you do accept American Express?'

'I'm sorry madam but we do not. Do you have any other type of Credit or debit card'

'Yes I do but not on me I'm afraid. I'll have to return another day'

'If madam would care to leave a deposit, I can put them by for you'

'Sorry but I have left my chequebook at home also,' she said handing back the boots.

'We also accept cash' he said flatly'

'Sorry, but without my cards I am unable to get cash from the dispenser' She praised herself for her quick thinking 'I'll return tomorrow with my visa card, goodbye'. Her legs felt like jelly as she left the shop. She knew this was the nearest she would ever get to owning the boots. She still lived with her parents 'But not for much longer' she told herself. Most of her allowance went on fares to and from work. Even though she would get expenses at the end of the month, money seemed to go nowhere. She sighed heavily. How would she ever afford her own place? 'Oh damn,' she said under her breath as the clock in the square struck two. 'I'd better get a move on or I'll be late'. She had no time to eat her sandwich and ran up the steps into the building where she worked for Zatman & Wolff, chartered accountants.

Ellie Lane, 19, was on a work experience programme at Zatman & Wolff. She worked 25 hours per week. Not only would this look good on her CV, but there was a real chance she could be taken on permanently at the end of her six-month placement. However, there were two flies in her ointment. Miranda Ingham, personal assistant to Anthony Zatman and Amelia Cheyney, personal assistant to Martin Wolff. Her initial interview had gone well with Mr Wolff and two days later she had been called for a second interview with Mr Zatman who was gruff and fired questions at her which made her nervous and stutter when she gave her answers. But he must have liked her, being the senior partner it was his final decision who to hire and the following Monday he rang her personally to offer her the placement and had been very kind and helpful on her first day, introducing her to all the staff, who were all very friendly. That is everyone except for Miranda and Amelia. They were both very attractive, 'In a sort of Cindy and Barbie way', Ellie had thought. Their suits were hand-made at Maurice Sedwell of Savile Row, their hair 'designed' at the Nicky Clarke Salon in Mayfair, and went everywhere together. She had been informed by the 'gofer' Joe Daniels, as he liked to call himself, on her first day.

******

'Ellie Lane, have you been looking in that shop

window again?' Miranda enquired, blocking the doorway.
'Not today, I went for a walk in the park'.
'Don't lie!' Miranda hissed, 'Amelia and I saw you going into Savoir-Faire. Buy the boots did you? Or were you chatting up the salesman?' She threw back her head and laughed.
Ellie tried to save face and said 'I tried them on and decided they were not for me' 'Out of your price range don't you mean dear? Why don't you try Shoes 4 U?, I'm sure you'll find something more suitable for your purse there'.
Ellie was seething inside But was lost for a suitable answer. 'Oh and by the way, Mr Zatman wants you to make three photocopies of this document, double-sided, and don't take all day about it, it has to go off in the post tonight' And with a toss of her long auburn hair, Miranda went back to her desk and started chatting on the phone to one of her equally obnoxious friends, Ellie guessed.
Five minutes later Amelia Cheyney waltzed in, she was a snob just like Miranda and the two of them were best friends. They both looked in Ellie's direction, Amelia said something out of earshot and they both laughed out loudly.
'Miranda where is the Mulalley file? I asked you for it before lunch!' Anthony Zatman bellowed. The colour drained from Miranda's face, 'I'm sorry Mr Zatman, I'll get it for you straight away' Ellie smiled wryly, at least someone could get one over on Miranda Ingham. She gave a little skip on her

way to the photocopier.

Ellie finished the photocopying and took it back to Miranda. 'Here are the copies you wanted Miranda' 'Why thank you' she said sweetly and stood up knocking her cup of coffee all over the papers. 'Oh, how clumsy of me! I'm so sorry. I guess you'll have to do it all over again won't you?' 'You did that on purpose Miranda' Ellie said. 'I certainly did not! Now go and copy them again while I get a cloth to mop up' Ellie felt the sting of tears in her eyes. Why was Miranda so spiteful? Ellie was no threat to her. It must be because she was the newcomer and not yet able to stand up for herself.

Five o'clock could not come quick enough for Ellie. The sun was still warm and she decided to go for a walk in Green Park before going back home. She would stop off for a coffee and danish to cheer herself up, but realised she was sixty pence short as she counted out her change, - Unless I dip into tomorrow's fares, she thought.
Just then alarm bells started ringing and a voice shouted 'Stop, thief!' Ellie saw a man running towards her and in his hands he had a pair of red boots, her boots!. Horrified, and taking the only action that she could, she swung her bag with all her might as the man tried to run by, and hit him in the face. Winded and surprised by the blow, he fell against the railings, dropping the boots, pausing just long enough for the policeman in

pursuit to catch up with him, pin him to the ground and handcuff his wrists.

Another policeman arrived with a policewoman who said to Ellie 'That was a brave thing you did love. I'm sure the manager of the shop will want to thank you personally'. 'Really, there's no need, I'm just glad I was in the right place, at the right time. I must rush or I'll miss my bus'.

Next morning everyone at the office was talking about the thwarted robbery. 'They say some girl stopped the thief dead in his tracks' Joe Daniels, said.

'She was just lucky the thief didn't have a knife on him or she may not have lived to tell the tale' Amelia said.

'And all for the sake of a pair of red boots I wouldn't give the time of day to' Miranda said.

'That's not what I heard' Joe said laughing, 'They didn't have a pair in the shop to fit your size seven feet more like it'

'Who ever heard of a shop that only caters for small sizes anyway' Miranda sniffed. 'I only went in there to chat up the gorgeous manager. I really had no interest in the boots at all'

'Turn you down then did he?' Joe asked teasingly.

'Just shut up Joe Daniels and get back to work. I'm sure you have post to be sorted', Miranda blazed.

Mr Zatman came out of his office and everyone immediately went to their positions. 'Well it seems

we have a hero in our midst' he said. 'Ellie, I believe it was you who foiled the thief. The manager of Savoir-Faire left this parcel and a note for you. Well done young lady, take the rest of the day off. Just make sure you are in bright and early tomorrow'
'Thank you Mr Zatman' Ellie said smiling.
'You?' Miranda said, 'I never would have believed it, you don't seem the type!' 'Never judge a book by its cover' Joe said. Miranda shot him a murderous look 'All right, all right, I'm going' he said, winking at Ellie.
Ellie put on her coat, she felt proud of herself for the first time in ages. But before she left, she opened the parcel and was unable to hide her astonishment. Inside were red boots, THE boots she had dreamed about all this time. She opened the enclosed letter and read,

'Dear Miss Lane, please accept this gift as a thank you from all the staff at Savoir-Faire. Not only did the thief steal the boots, he also seized our bank takings for the day. On a personal note, I recognised you the day you came into the shop. I often saw you looking in the window at the boots, they seem a fitting reward for your bravery. May you wear them in good health. As a further thank-you, I have booked a table at Giuseppes, for this Friday at 8p.m., when I hope to get to know you better.

Yours sincerely, James Fielding - Manager'

THE MAN IN THE GREY SUIT

The man stood alone. A dark, solitary figure against the bright dawn sky.

When he first came to this place, his grey pin-striped suit, although not new, was in good condition. His felt trilby hat made him look dapper, so he'd been told, and his black patent shoes had shone.

Now, his once tailored suit was almost threadbare with a hole at the knee. His cracked patent shoes were tied with broken laces and he no longer wore the hat. His yellow hair was unkempt and missing in patches, his eyes sad and weary from things he had witnessed over the years. Yet still he stood here, day after day. In good weather as well as foul. In sunshine, wind, rain and even snow. 'For what else is there for one such as I?' he asked himself. He knew no better and was far too old to change his ways now.

He recalled how he had once been respected, but this was no longer so. The schoolchildren could be really cruel, especially the boys, especially that little brat, Johnny Vincent. Yes, he was their ringleader, jeering the others on, and like the pied piper they followed his every move.

One day last summer he had even resorted to violence!

'What was the date?' he asked himself, annoyed that his memory wasn't as it used to be. June sometime ... yes, that had to be right because the day had been hot, he remembered, and the previous evening not dark until ten o'clock

He recalled the day in perfect detail, as if it were yesterday.

He had been standing in this very spot. The hot sun on his face had cheered him. Some people had remarked it was too hot. Tut, tut ... he thought. There's no pleasing some folk. Why, hadn't it rained every single day the week before and the same people had moaned about that?

Then his thoughts returned to Johnny Vincent. Johnny Vincent had golden, curly hair. No doubt his mother's blue-eyed boy who could do no wrong. But HE knew different ... Oh yes. Knew what an evil little monster he really was. It must have been about four o'clock when the boys had arrived, still in school uniform and in a cloud of dust. Johnny Vincent rode on his shiny red BMX bike, tie askew and his best black shoes scuffed, no doubt from wearing them whilst playing football or kicking some unsuspecting dumb animal.

'Look. He's still there standing in that damn field!' Johnny Vincent shouted.

Hadn't the boy's mother taught him not to swear! Hmm ... probably would take no notice of her even if she had tried. She was probably at her wits' end, not knowing what to do with her little Johnny!

'Hand me up a rock and I'll see if I can knock his hat off.'

He'd stood there defiant and unblinking, not believing for one moment that Johnny would actually throw the rock. The first missile whizzed past his left ear, narrowly missing it. The second found its target and the hat fell to the ground.

The boys squealed with delight. Whooping, and no doubt because he was the centre of attention, Johnny jumped up and down.

The man could not believe what had just happened. Did the young no longer have any respect for their elders? Apparently not. Johnny picked up another rock. One of the boys feigned concern and tried to stop him by saying 'Hey Johnny. I think we should go home now. Your mum and mine will be hopping mad if they find out what we've done!'

'Hold on Pete. I just need to take one last shot and wipe that stupid look off his face.'

Enough is enough now, boys, the man thought. You've had your fun. Pete is right, you should go home, trying to stare Johnny down.

The rock had whizzed past his other ear, but he stood his ground, not wanting to show the fear he felt in his heart. Crash! The sound of breaking glass as the stone hit the farmer's window.

'Bloody hell,' Pete Blamey yelled. 'Leggit before old farmer Craddick comes out with his shotgun.'

'Damn scoundrels. I know where you live!' Farmer

Craddick shouted after them. 'I'm letting the dogs loose'.

But the boys had long gone before the farmer could carry out his threat, pedalling as fast as their legs would go.

Oh how funny that vision had been, he thought, laughing until it hurt.

The farmer had been kind. Showing his concern he'd said, 'I'm so sorry, old fella. No respect for anything those damn kids. I'd better board up the window and pick up the glass before the dogs cut their paws.'

The very next morning, before school, Mrs Vincent, along with Johnny, had appeared at the farmer's door.

'I'm so sorry, Farmer Craddick,' she said. 'Johnny will pay for the damage out of his pocket money. And as a further apology I told him ... er ... I mean he wants to give you his favourite baseball cap for the hat he may have damaged yesterday.'

What? the man thought, astonished, hearing every word of the conversation. Surely she doesn't think I'd wear a baseball cap!

'That won't be necessary,' Farmer Craddick replied.

'Oh yes, it is,' Mrs Vincent insisted. 'Johnny, come and say sorry!'

'Sorry. Farmer Craddick,' he mumbled.

'What are you saying? Speak up boy, I can't hear you.'

'I said I'm sorry.'

'Well, it's not just me you should be apologising to. Go on down the field and say your apologies there also.'

'No way!' Johnny cried out. 'That old man gives me the creeps!' and in the next instant he sped off towards the school building, riding his red bicycle.

It was also agreed between Mrs Vincent and Farmer Craddick that Johnny, along with the rest of his gang, would help out on the farm, for one week, feeding the hens, collecting eggs and doing chores wherever the farmer saw fit.

The man had watched each day from a safe distance in the field, a wry smile crossing his face as he thought, How sweet retribution is!

The farmer had given the man the denim baseball cap. 'It will do Johnny Vincent good to see it on your head every time he comes past my field,' the farmer chuckled.

There had been no further incident with Johnny Vincent, Pete Blamey or any of the other children since that time. In fact, all the man ever saw of them nowadays was a blur and a cloud of dust as they whizzed past on their bikes, either to or from school; they never even glanced in his direction.

The hot sun rose high into the azure blue sky and the man's thoughts returned to the present. 'At least the baseball cap shelters these old eyes from the sun and I don't have to squint,' he said to himself.

Often. over the past few weeks, as if by some sort of sixth sense, he felt his time was coming to an end. At times he had thought he wasn't ready to go just yet and at other times he thought how he would embrace it, yearning for his end to come quickly. 'Everything is so different from when I was young,' he said, recalling that when Farmer Craddick had first been married, two strong shire horses had pulled the plough behind them in the field. 'Now those ugly yellow machines have taken over,' the man groaned, referring to the farmer's combine harvester.

The farmer's pretty daughter used to come down into the field sometimes and eat her sandwich with him, telling him of her day at school and how she had fallen out with her best friend, Marian.

She'd tied a pale-green scarf around his neck, kissed him on the forehead and said 'There, you look handsome again' and ran off back to the farm when her mother had called out, 'It's time to come in and do your homework.' But now the sweet child was grown into a woman and was getting married to the village doctor in September.

The man felt a twinge in his left knee and knew without even having to look at the gathering clouds that rain was on its way.

As the first clap of thunder rumbled in the distance, the pain and numbness crept up his left arm. 'What should I do? What should I do?' he cried out in alarm as the rain began to fall steadily.

He heard a voice in his head: 'Don't fight it,' it said. 'Do not be afraid, for I have come to take you home.'

'But I am not yet ready!' the man said. 'I have still work to do and not said my goodbyes'

'There is no need to fret,' the voice said. 'Your work is done. A replacement will be found to carry out your work.'

At that moment the clouds parted and a ray of sunshine shone down to the earth.

'Are you ready?' the voice asked.

The old man looked up and saw a disembodied hand reaching out to him. 'Yes,' he whispered, as he felt himself being lifted into the air.

A sudden gust of wind blew his lifeless body to the ground. It blew the baseball cap from his head and tossed it all the way to the farmer's back door.

The farmer's wife looked out of the back window and shouted out 'Oh my goodness, the wind has blown the old man over!'

Farmer Craddick put his arm around his wife's shoulder and said teasingly, 'All this fuss over an old scarecrow. I hope you show as much concern when it's my turn to go.'

INVASION

'Joanne..... Please help me!'.

The voice sounded far away. I opened my eyes and looked at the clock on the bedside cupboard. 2a.m. Had I been dreaming?

This time there was a desperate pounding on the front door, followed by the same anxious plea.

'Joanne, please wake up and help me'.

I threw back the bedclothes, slipped on my dressing gown and ran down the stairs.

'What's up mom?' My daughter, Sophie called out over the bannister, rubbing the sleep from her eyes.

'I don't know honey. Your aunt Val is at the front door she seems upset. Why don't you go back to bed, you have school in the morning.

'I hope Theo's OK', she said, sitting on the stairs, hugging her knees.

'I'm sure it's something and nothing'.

I opened the door and Val fell into the hall. 'He says he's gone to find his father', she said, stifling a sob.

'Who?' I asked.

'Don't be stupid Joanne!' she said crossly. 'Theo who else?'

'You mean he has gone to Melbourne?'

'Oh Joanne!' she wailed, 'I haven't been entirely truthful with you'.

Floods of tears came now, like the bursting of a

damn. All I could do was hug her and hope her body would soon stop shaking long enough for her to explain what had happened.

Sophie ran down the stairs, 'What's happened to Theo?' she asked.

'All in good time', I said, 'Be a sweetie and put the kettle on'

Val had stopped crying and regained some composure

'A cup of hot chocolate would be nice' she said, ruffling Sophie's hair.

'O.K., I'll make some chocolate for all three of us. But I'm coming straight back to find out what's happened to Theo'.

I led Val into the living room, she was now shivering and drew her coat around her. I flicked on the switch for the gas fire and turned to Val. She looked much older than her forty years.

'We should be out there, looking for Theo' she said.

'We're going nowhere until you explain what happened'

Val breathed a deep, painful sigh and began to explain.

'You remember the night of Friday 13th October 1995?

Why was she bringing that night up now? 'Of course, I remember. I could hardly forget. Although it's been a while since I've thought about it'

'Have you ever told Sophie,?' she asked.

'Surprisingly not!' I answered. 'I don't want her to think her mother is mad'.

'It's all the secrecy that's led to Theo running away!' she exclaimed.

'What does this have to do with that night in 1995?'

Sophie came into the room carrying a tray, three cups of chocolate and a plate of shortbread biscuits. Val and I fell silent.

'I'm not going back to bed', she declared 'And I'm not a child, so I want to know why Theo has run away'

Val took hold of one of Sophie's hands and patted the seat next to her on the sofa, indicating for me to sit next to her.

'This may seem hard for you to believe, but I swear to you, both of you it's all true' Val took a few sips from one of the mugs of chocolate. She cleared her throat and continued with her explanation.

'Friday 13th October 1995 was an unusually warm day for the time of year. Your mother and I and Rachel Thomas, a friend of ours from school, had been talking about going to see this film we'd wanted to see for ages. The Bridges of Madison County. It was still on at the multiview cinema in Barnet and Rachel had bought three tickets for us to go that evening. It was to be a girls night out you see. Just us three, no men'

'That's usually what a girls night out means!' I quipped, sarcastically. Val licked her lips, ignoring my irritation, she took a sip from her mug and resumed the tale.

'It was still early enough when the film ended so we all got into my car and headed for the Red Lion pub. We sat at the bar and got into a conversation with the head barman, who fancied your mum like mad, he invited us to stay for a drink after closing time'

'I remember all this' I said, 'Is there any point to this story?'

'I'm recounting the story for Sophie. As you said she hadn't heard it before'

'Yeah mum, and if you keep interrupting it will take even longer for Aunt Val to finish!'

'OK..... sorry. Please, Val, continue'.

'I was only drinking orange juice, but your mum and Rachel were on Vodka and lemonade and were quite tipsy, with your mum promising to ring the barman the following week, which she had no intention of doing as she was engaged to your dad. We left the pub after midnight in high spirits, your mum and Rachel started singing as soon as they got back in the car. We travelled along the St Albans Road and were somewhere near the Knebworth Golf Club, because I'd just seen the sign to turn off, both passengers were asleep by then. As I approached the roundabout I was momentarily blinded by a dazzling white light. Next thing, the car's engine with all of the electrical equipment went out. I shouted for your mum and Rachel to wake up, because I was frightened and didn't know what the hell was happening. Rachel rolled down the back window and looked out. 'Oh my God, what's that?' she cried. We all looked out and saw a huge cylindrical shaped craft in the sky, with pulsating lights which changed from red, to blue, to white and back again. We just stared at this thing and then back at one another. I told them to roll up the window and lock all the doors, I was scared and taking no chances. Rachel started to cry and I grabbed her hand and your mothers telling them both to close their eyes and breathe deeply, like I'd been shown at Yoga, counting the breath to steady our nerves. The next thing I remember was the car's engine and lights spluttering back to life, when we opened our eyes it was dark again, with no sign of the craft. The most amazing thing is that it all appeared to take place in a short space of time, we looked at our watches which had stopped at exactly 2a.m. but when the radio suddenly came on with the 5 o'clock news we were all amazed, we had lost three hours!'

'I don't believe a word of it' Sophie said. 'You must have dreamt it all when you fell asleep.

'What, all three of us had the same dream, at the same time do you mean? That takes a bit of believing don't you think?'

'It's no harder to believe than what you just told me. Is this why Theo has run away? He didn't believe you either!'

'Actually, you are wrong. He did believe me and that's why he's gone'.

'I'm getting dressed. I want to go look for Theo'

Val grabbed Sophie by the arm. 'Don't you think I've already looked in all your 'secret' places?. Rung every school friend?. Sit down and let me finish, now that I've started!'

It was a command which Sophie obeyed. A sudden chill filled the room, so I turned up another notch on the gas fire.

Sophie pushed up the sleeve of her pyjamas. I could clearly see the red marks left by Val's fingers. But I just sat there like a dummy instead of defending my daughter.

'You hurt me!' Sophie scowled.

'I'm sorry' Val said, 'But I didn't want you to run off too. May I continue?'

'I guess so. Especially if the end leads us to Theo's whereabouts!'

There was something in Val's manner which made me question if I really wanted to hear the rest of this story, so I said, 'You are clearly upset Val and I don't blame you, but this reminiscing isn't helping us to find your son!'

'Please Joanne..... sit!' Val stared me down until I

complied.

'My pounding heart began to slow and the panic I'd felt earlier subsided a little, so I slowly opened my eyes, hoping that everything had gone back to normal. It hadn't, the craft was still there and then something happened that simply terrified me. A sphere of blue-white light came hurtling towards the car and exploded just short of the bonnet. When I recovered from the shock, I was horrified to see the car surrounded by beings!'

'What did they look like?' Sophie cried, her eyes wide with wonder.

'They were quite small' Val continued, 'about the size of a six-year-old child. They wore some sort of silver suit. Their heads appeared to be too large for their bodies and their eyes were the shape of a cats, but much, much bigger and black in colour. They had three fingers on each gloved hand and one of them pulled on the door handle, trying to get inside!'

'Oh blimey! Were you scared? Did mum and Rachel not see this too?'

'No, they were both out cold. I tried shaking them but neither one responded I was terrified. The next thing I knew, I was outside the car standing in the road, the beings had hold of my arms and I could not move! A shaft of light came from the craft as a door opened and out stepped another being. I could not make out its features at first as he was silhouetted against the glare'.

'You said 'he'. How did you know it was a 'he'. I asked, hardly able to believe my ears.

'Because he looked just like Clint Eastwood'

I could contain myself no longer and burst out laughing 'Oh Val, you must have been dreaming'

'If you've quite finished, may I continue?'

I nodded my head, unable to speak a word for fear of laughing out loud again.

'The man....being...spoke to me with his mind. He said not to be afraid, he wasn't here to hurt anyone and explained he could appear before me in any guise he chose, so as not to alarm me. He said his name was Xianthon and he was a supreme being on his planet, the little creatures were just workers. It was all too much for me, I must have fainted. The next thing I remember was being back in the car, the radio suddenly coming to life, and your mum and Rachel saying how cold they were and could we please just go home?'

'Why did you not tell us this before?' I asked

'At first, I thought I had dreamt it. Just as Sophie suggested. Then when no-one believed our story, friends and family even suggesting we had done something really wild that night and concocted the tale between us just to cover up, I just clammed up. You know how bad it got Joanne. That's why Rachel went to live in Canada with her aunt.'

'Yes but why didn't you tell us?..... me? We had

been there with you?'

'I could never find the right time. Then a few months later I found out I was pregnant, I had to tell Jack. He asked me who the father was, I couldn't tell him. 'But I thought Jack was Theo's father. That when you told him you were pregnant he just legged it to Australia because he didn't want the responsibility?'

'Jack is not Theo's father. I wouldn't tell him who the father was because I couldn't believe it myself. He took my silence as an admission to having a lover behind his back. It was easier to let him believe this. He finished things right there and then, and when the job came up in Melbourne he jumped at the chance and took it. Even phoned to tell me, said I'd broken his heart'

'If Jack is not Theo's father, then who is?' I asked.

Val let out a long, slow sigh, then replied 'I was not pregnant before the encounter with the aliens, nor was I romantically linked with any other man, other than Jack at the time. Draw your own conclusions. I had to'

'I can hardly believe any of this' I said

'Why not? You were there'.

'Yes, I know..... but..... how is this possible?'

'Really Joanne, you gave birth to a beautiful daughter. I don't need to teach you the facts of life!'

'Yes..... but you are saying you do not remember the encounter aren't you?'

'I've told you everything I remember. The result of this 'encounter', as you so delicately put it, was my son Theo'.

'You told all this to Theo and he didn't believe you either' Sophie said 'No wonder he ran away!'

'On the contrary. He DID believe me, said so in his note. This is why he ran away'

'I can't listen to any more of this garbage!' Sophie said as she ran sobbing from the room.

'Shouldn't you go after her?' Val asked

'No, let her calm down. It's a lot to take in. She'll be OK' I replied. 'How did you feel when you.....um.....realised you were pregnant?'

'Bewildered. Violated. Invaded, to name but a few and then dread. I wondered what the child would look like. It took me ages to have my first scan and when I asked the nurse if everything was 'normal', she laughed and said "of course, ten fingers, ten toes and a strong heartbeat!" However, I was not convinced. Not until I held my son in my arms for the first time and could see for myself'.

'I still don't understand why you went through all this on your own'

'But I didn't, I had your support. How could I confess when you were pregnant yourself with Sophie? I couldn't lay all that at your door. Besides, from the moment I saw my son I fell in love with him. I realised quickly that he was a gift from God, no matter who his father was. The name I chose for him, Theodore, actually means gift from God'

'Oh Val, you must be going out of your mind with worry. What did you actually tell Theo?'

'Everything. He was stunned but never questioned me in any way. When I enquired if he was OK he just said 'Can I go to my room now?' a few minutes later I heard his TV playing the theme tune to his favourite programme. I went up an hour later with some food and was asked to leave it outside his door, I figured it was his way of dealing with the news and was not unduly worried. I woke up around 1a.m., the TV was still on. I went to his room, knocked on the door and said 'Honey, you have school in the morning, please turn off the TV and get some sleep' There was no answer and when I realised that the tray of food was still outside his door I went in and found the note on his pillow'

'Have you contacted the police?'

'And tell them what? That my son's father is an alien and he has run off to find him? Yeah, that would go down a storm at their local watering hole don't you think? They would laugh at me all the way to the funny farm!'.

'What are you going to do then?' I asked.

The first light of dawn crept across the sky and Val replied, 'We have been talking all night and I still don't have a clue'

'Didn't you say all of this took place on Deards End Lane?' Sophie asked as she descended the stairs.

'Yes, close to the Knebworth Golf Club' Val replied

'Then it seems the most obvious place to start. Mum, get dressed and get the car out. I want to know what's happened to my best mate'

Ten minutes later we climbed into my battered old Volvo and headed for the motorway.

The pale, watery sun rose into a cloudless blue sky. Trees and houses flashed by in a blur and Val shouted, 'I'd rather we got there in one piece Joanne, slow down before you get pulled over by the police!'

'OK, OK..... Sorry, I wasn't watching the speedometer' I said, easing my foot off the accelerator. Sophie sat in silence. Every now and then wiping a tear from her eye, all the while clutching at a yellow teddy bear with a red tee-shirt Theo had given her on her last birthday.

Val spoke again, 'Throughout his life, as Theo has been growing up I have noticed small differences to other kids, nothing major. He has an uncanny sixth sense.

'What do you mean by that?' I asked

'For instance, in the case of Old Mrs Taylor's cat who went missing. When Theo found out he asked her if she had any personal item belonging to the cat that he could hold'

'I remember that!' Sophie said excitedly 'She gave Theo an odd look but went away and a few minutes later came back with a fluffy mouse!. Theo held it in his hand, closed his eyes for a few seconds then said that the cat was locked in a neighbour's house. We had to wait all day until the neighbour came home, then, sure enough, the missing cat was found. It had followed their cat in through the cat flap and must have got frightened because it was crouched in a corner behind the TV!'

Val put an arm around Sophie's shoulder and kissed the top of her head. 'I know how much you love Theo. Don't worry, we'll find him'

'There's the turn off for the Knebworth Golf club!' Sophie cried eagerly. I turned the Volvo a little too sharply to the right, but this time there was no chastisement. I pulled into the first layby. 'What now?' I asked.

'I'm not really sure' Val replied. Minutes later there was a knock on the back window. We shrieked in unison and turned to see Theo standing on the hard shoulder. 'Sorry if I startled you' he said. Val and Sophie jumped out, both hugging and kissing Theo at the same time. 'We were so worried!' Sophie said. I got out of the car and said to Theo, 'I've never been so glad to see anyone in my whole life!', playfully ruffling his hair.

'I knew you'd come. But I wasn't quite sure if you'd get here before I left', he said.

'Where are going?' Sophie asked. 'We've only just found you!'

'Mum, I was dumbfounded when you told me about my father, but I knew you would never lie to me. I realised that I had to find him, but he actually found me' Theo said, turning to Val. 'My father says that he fears for our safety. I mean the safety of humankind, our planet, the way we abuse it and take it for granted. He will teach me many things I would never learn on earth, how to reverse the effects of what we have done before it is too late and we are lost forever. He says that I must get your permission first, mum to travel back with him. If you really don't want me to go, then I will stay'.

A sudden wind blew up rustling the trees and a tall man with brown hair stepped out from behind one. He had a kind face with eyes just like Theo's, but he made no attempt to come closer.

'Must I make up my mind now? ' Val asked weakly.

'Yes, or he will leave without me'.

You are my whole world Theo, but I would never stand in your way. If you believe you must do this then go with my blessing'.

'Thanks mum' Theo said. Mother and son hugged for a long time, tears streaming down their faces

'Hey, what about me?' Sophie said running to Theo. 'I'm gonna lose my best friend!' 'I won't be gone forever Sophes. I will be able to communicate once father teaches me how.' 'Make sure you do or you'll have me to answer to!' I said, 'C'mere and give me a hug'.

I must go' Theo Said. 'Wait, please take pooh bear with you. You can give him back to me when you return' Sophie said, choking back tears. 'Thanks Sophes. I will look after him for you. Will you take care of mum for me please aunt Joanne? Make sure she's not too lonely'

'You don't have to ask Theo, please take care of yourself'

'I love you all, but it's time for me to leave now' Theo turned and headed for the tree where the man still stood.

'I can't imagine life without him' Val whispered to me, stifling a sob. 'He'll be back one day and who knows what he'll be able to teach us' I replied, feigning a smile. Theo turned to waive, we watched until he was out of sight. A few minutes later, a sound reached our ears like the whirring of a hundred helicopter blades as a sphere of bright light sped overhead, in a flash, it was gone.

WEB OF DECEPTION

‘Oh what a tangled web we weave, when first we practice to deceive’

This is the second time since breakfast, the phrase has come into my head, but I push it to the back of my mind as I climb aboard the crowded bus.

'134, to Tottenham Court Road', the recorded voice tells me as I take out my magazine and feign interest. 'North Circular Road,' 'How does the voice know where we are?', I ponder. 'Does it count the number of traffic lights since North Finchley? Some artificial intelligence ready to take over the planet when the time is right?'

‘A tangled web,’ my mind shouts at me again. 'Go away', I say under my breath. Perhaps if I read something in the magazine it will divert my thoughts. I turn to my horoscope page, this is always good for a laugh, but the words leap off the page at me. ‘Relationships may suffer this month if you are not completely honest with your partner.’ I quickly turn to the crossword puzzle as The Voice informs passengers 'Highgate Station'.

One down three letters, ‘an untruth’. 'Lie' I whisper. 'Is the universe trying to give me a message', I wonder.

'Waterlow Road' the voice continues as the driver pulls into the next stop. But no-one gets on or off the bus. The boy in front of me hums an incomprehensible tune and taps his toes in time to his I-pod.

'Kentish Town Station'

'Cheer up love. Why so long a face on such a lovely morning?' I look up into a brown, weather-beaten face, with ice-blue eyes, crinkled at the corners. The woman's coat has seen better days and she is wearing purple socks. I almost laugh out loud as I notice she is still wearing slippers, complete with pom-poms, but I manage to stifle it with a hand over my mouth.

'That's better. you're quite pretty when you smile' she remarks, sitting next to me, treating me to an almost toothless grin. 'How far are you going?' she asks.

'To Camden Town', I reply. 'I thought I would do some shopping in the market'

'What, and get your purse pinched for your trouble?. The weather forecast is changeable for the rest of the week. Why not take yourself up to Regents Park'.

'Because I don't want to be alone with my thoughts', I say to myself, but to her, I say 'I might just do that' as The Voice informs us that we are at 'St

Andrew‘s church'

'I‘m on my way to pick up Bobby' She tells me.

'Bobby?' I ask.

'Sorry dear, my cat. He is 9 years old and at the Veterinary College. Very ill he's been and my only friend, or so I thought. When my neighbours heard of my dilemma they made a collection so I could afford the vet's bill. Still, some decent people left in the world'.

I feel guilty now for laughing at her ridiculous slippers. She obviously has more important things on her mind.

She continues, 'Turns out Gloria and I share a love of cats, she lives at 141. We've become good friends.

'That's nice', is all I can manage to say.

'Camden Town Station', she says drowning out the voice, 'My stop and yours, but we are heading in different directions. So nice to have met you love'.

A tear pricks at the back of my eyes as we step from the bus and she shuffles along, humming a little tune.

'She is right', I decide. 'The day is too nice to spend it shopping'. I walk up Park Way heading for Regents Park. 'Practice to deceive,' I mumble entering the little café.

'What's that love?' the girl asks me from behind the counter.

'Cappuccino, please. Oh, and a cream slice'.

'Coming up. That will be £4.75 pence, please'

I pay for my purchases and head for a table outside in the sunshine and before I even sit down my thoughts turn to Steven Bailey.

Steven Bailey, 34, sales executive, with smiling brown eyes and dark-blonde hair. Steven Bailey, charismatic, magnetic, and asking me at every opportunity to go away with him for a weekend, even though he knows I am getting married this summer. I must admit, I am very tempted and my head is full of thoughts of him, especially since his last invitation to Brussels and the all expenses paid business trip.

'Why not', I ask myself 'One last fling whilst I'm still single. Don't men do it all the time?', I justify to myself.

As I toy with the idea of phoning him, a huge black spider runs across the table and stops, dead centre. Momentarily distracted I watch the creature. I have no fear of spiders but just the same I would not like it crawling over me and I shiver at this idea. It runs around the top of the table as if not sure where to go. The waitress from the café comes over with a newspaper and swiftly scoops up the spider and empties it into some flowers nearby.

'Some people would believe that to be an omen', she

says to me

'Good or bad?' I ask.

'Er..... Sorry love, I dunno' she answers, shrugging her shoulders. She picks up the empty plates and goes back into the café.

Breathing deeply to calm my nerves, I take my mobile from my handbag. Hesitating I look at my watch, 11.52 a.m., 'What if he's in a meeting?' I ask myself 'Then you leave a message' comes the reply. With shaking hands, I begin punching in his number and almost drop the phone as it beep-beeps. It's a voicemail from one of my colleagues at the office.

'You missed all the fun this morning' she chirps 'Seems like Steven Bailey has been having an affair with the boss's wife. Almost came to blows they did. He was given his marching orders soon after. Aren't you glad you never got mixed up with him? Then why would you with a gorgeous fiancée like yours! Bye for now, see you in the morning'

The old lady was right, sometimes we don't realise what we have on our own doorstep. The desire for what we don't have prevents us from appreciating and enjoying what we do have - right now..... And I came very close to throwing it all away.

FORDWYCH HOUSE

'And the Master Bedroom has a magnificent view of Hampstead Heath', Michael said.

'I believe you but it's not me you have to convince' Cathy replied.

He was determined to make the sale today, had been trying to offload this house for three months now, but every time he thought he had made a sale, the buyer would pull out at the last minute.

'Today is going to be my lucky day, Cathy', he added, buttering a slice of toast. 'I'll take you on that weekend to Cornwall I have been promising you'.

'You won't mind if I don't hold my breath will you?' she replied, sarcastically.

'Aw, c'mon hon, give a guy a break. This is just what Mr & Mrs Robbins have been looking for.'

He's certainly persistent - Cathy thought, - So maybe I will give him the benefit of the doubt, just for once, 'OK, I want to see this one with my own eyes' she said to a surprised Michael, not mentioning the real reason she had said yes was the promise of a pub lunch.

The house was indeed splendid. Mr & Mrs Robbins followed Michael in and out of each room chatting happily and nodding their heads in approval. 'Now, if you'd care to come this way, I'll show you the newly refurbished kitchen', Michael said. Mr & Mrs Robbins followed obediently, but Cathy had other plans and decided to do some exploring of her own.

The passageway which led to the back of the house was dark, the walls painted a sickly shade of brown. 'Yuk, whoever the previous owner was sure didn't have good taste in interior decoration' Cathy said to herself as she searched blindly for the light switch, at the same time wondering why the rest of the house had been modernised whilst seemingly leaving this part untouched. 'Yes!' she cheered as she found the light switch, but with a flicker and a pop, it went out again. 'Damn!', she muttered under her breath, 'Now I'll have to grope my way in this gloom'.

As her eyes became accustomed to the half-light she could make out a mirror on the wall. A glimmer of sun shone in through the back door, outlining a coat rack with a man's Fedora hat on one of the pegs. Curious she took it down and wondered who it could belong to as the house had stood empty for some time. It was made of grey felt and perfectly clean with a black band around it. She returned it to the stand and walked towards the back door. She turned the handle and was surprised to find it unlocked, the door opened silently, not a creak or a groan as she had expected from such an old house.

The sun had broken through the clouds and it was unusually warm for mid-November. Cathy smiled gratefully and closed her eyes as the sun generously stroked her skin. She imagined she could hear music, it reminded her of her father whom she hadn't thought of in a long while. Tears pricked the back of her eyes, she wiped them away quickly with a tissue. Squinting in the bright light, she realised that she had not imagined it, there was definitely music coming from somewhere. She turned her head in its direction and was pleasantly surprised to find a well-kept lawn, with roses still in bloom and a familiar tune coming through some open French windows. It had reminded her of her father because it was his favourite, 'Little Brown Jug' by Glen Miller. She recalled her father had told her how he met her mother at the Lyceum Ballroom in London's Strand and had jived with her for the first time to this very tune. Cathy walked towards the French windows, a strong smell of coffee coming from inside.

'Hello,' a man said as she approached. Startled, she stopped in her tracks.

'Oh, I am so sorry' Cathy said, 'I didn't realise there was anyone living here' The man was tall with sleeked-back black hair and a small moustache. He wore the traditional blue uniform of the Royal Air Force. He smiled, showing even white teeth.

'You must be new to the neighbourhood', he laughed, 'This house has been in my family forever!'

'I'm Cathy Fenton' she said, regaining her composure and extending a hand.

'How charming' the man said as he took her hand and kissed it.

Cathy felt a blush rise up from her neck and creep into her cheeks.

'What an amazing shade of crimson', the man teased. 'Sorry, my name is Roger Fordwych and I am at your service ma'am' he gave a small salute and added 'won't you join me for a cup of coffee or can I tempt you to a glass of sherry?'

'Coffee would be perfect' Cathy replied.

Roger disappeared through the French windows, returning a few minutes later with a cup of steaming coffee on a silver tray with cream, sugar and an assortment of biscuits.

'I thought it best to bring a variety' he said referring to the biscuits, 'As I'm not sure what your preference is'

'Thank you', Cathy said taking a cream wafer 'Will you join me?'

'Yes thanks, I will. This is indeed a rare treat drinking black-market coffee with a pretty girl on a sunny afternoon'

Cathy laughed at his strange choice of words. - What does he mean by black-market? - she wondered. Perhaps the coffee had been brought into the country without paying the fair traders a decent wage?. Oh well, she wouldn't dwell on it this time. Roger was so pleasant and she found herself enjoying his attention.

'Tell me about yourself' he urged.

'Nothing exciting' Cathy replied. 'I am a reporter for our local newspaper. But it's mostly about local fetes and who's won the cutest baby competition, I'm afraid'.

'I have never met a lady reporter before. What a sheltered life I must have led!' Roger joked.

'And what about you?' Cathy asked 'Flown any planes lately?'

A dark shadow crossed Roger's face and the light faded from his blue eyes.

'Forgive me if I am being too inquisitive' Cathy threw at him.

'Not at all. Not at all. It's just a sore topic. Some of my best friends are probably flying over Germany as we speak, but I am unable to join them as my lungs have suffered smoke inhalation. So now all I'm fit for is a desk job!' he said bitterly. Cathy could sense his pain as she reached out to touch his sad face.

'Don't listen to me' Roger said 'Just feeling sorry for myself. Would you care for some more coffee? And how about a plate of sandwiches also?'

Cathy's tummy rumbled, 'You are spoiling me!' she said

'Well, a pretty gal deserves to be spoilt. I'll be back before you know it' Roger said, winking at her. Cathy sat back in her chair, enjoying the sunshine and Roger's company, she closed her eyes and soon drifted off to sleep.

She awoke some time later. The sun had disappeared, it was overcast and had begun to rain. Cathy looked about her, there was no sign of Roger, the once opened French windows were now closed and rosebuds lay dead upon the ground. She stood and pulled up the collar of her jacket as a chilly wind sprang up from nowhere. Cathy walked to the French windows and tried the rusted handle, but it was locked and a pane of glass was broken, she had not noticed this before. She knocked on the windows and called out 'Roger, are you there?' All was quiet save for the wind which whipped and stung at her face. Once more, 'Roger, please open the doors.' Still no response. Puzzled she decided to head back into the house to see if she could find Michael, but she could not drive Roger from her mind and the bizarre events of that afternoon.

'Cathy darling, there you are, I was beginning to worry about you'. Michael said upon seeing her. 'Where on earth have you been? Mr & Mrs Robbins have gone away to think things over, but it all seems very promising'

'I went for a stroll in the garden and dozed off in a chair', Cathy said smoothing down her skirt, now unsure if what happened earlier had been a manifestation of her subconscious. She recalled how as a child she would wake from a nightmare convinced it had been real until her father came to her room to comfort her, assuring her that she was just dreaming. They had been so close before he died and suddenly she remembered it was coming up to the fifth anniversary of his passing. 'Now it all makes sense' she said aloud.

Michael had not heard what she said and now he spoke to her. 'Look what Mrs Robbins found in an old chest in the attic. It's a copy of the Hampstead & Highgate Press, dated 8th May 1945'.

An article caught Cathy's attention, she snatched the newspaper and with trembling hands read:

'Today, the World War II Allies formally accepted the unconditional surrender of the armed forces of Nazi Germany and the end of Adolph Hitler's Third Reich. Whilst the rest of the country celebrated, a small funeral was held for the only son of Lord and Lady Fordwych. Flight Lieutenant Roger Fordwych, 30, last week lost his long battle with lung cancer.....'

Cathy looked at the clear, black and white photo of the man, which accompanied the article. He was seated in a rose garden, smartly attired in RAF uniform, and grey Fedora hat, his familiar face smiled out at her. An ice-cold sensation crawled up her spine and goose-bumps appeared on her arms.

'Are you OK, Cath?. You've turned very pale!'

Michael asked.

She regained some self-control and saw the look of concern on Michael's face. 'I haven't eaten since breakfast and suddenly felt light-headed. That's all silly!' 'Then I'd better take you to the pub like I promised, before you keel over', he teased.

THE GIRL IN THE BLACK & WHITE PHOTOGRAPH

At the stroke of midnight I got up and listened, no sounds, my parents must be asleep. I hastily dressed in black tee-shirt, black Jeans and black trainers. I opened my bedroom door as quietly as possible and made my way downstairs to the kitchen. I grabbed the flashlight, tiptoed into the hall and out the front door, putting the key in my pocket. I looked at my watch, 12.15; I was to meet the others at the top of the road at 12.30. The air was still and hot, not having cooled down much after the blistering heat of the day. I got to the top of the road and the others were already there. 'Are you certain you saw her leave' I asked my friend John whose persuasions had gathered us here. 'Yes. You've already asked me that question'. We walked along slowly until we reached the house. It looked eerie in the moonlight, the big tree in the front garden seemed to take on a different shape, like a giant it loomed, with its arms stretched heavenward. John opened the gate; it creaked and sounded as loud as a gunshot to me. I looked at the neighbouring houses; no lights came on, no twitching curtains or inquisitive faces at the window. I let out a long exhalation of breath and saw that the others were already at the front door. I hurried up the path and asked 'How do we get inside?' 'Easy' John said. 'I have a key.' 'How did you get that?' I asked. 'You ask too many questions'

John replied shoving a hand into his back pocket. I shrugged my shoulders at the other two but they said nothing following John into the house. I closed the door behind me. 'Keep flashlights turned towards the floor when near any windows' John said. I wandered into the living room and sat in a high back chair. I could hear someone in the next room opening and closing drawers and cupboard doors. Footsteps ascended the stairs which creaked and groaned their protest. I turned on the flashlight, it reflected off a photograph on the dresser. Curious, I walked across the room to take a better look. It was an old black and white photograph of a young man in a uniform with wings on the pocket. I recognized it at once, my father had told me his grandfather had been in the R.A.F. and had shown me a photograph very similar to this one. I wondered who the man was. I opened the top drawer and found a photograph album. I took it back to the high-backed chair and looked through the pages. There were more photographs of the man in uniform and also in ordinary clothing. Pictures of the man on his own, with an older couple and one kissing the cheek of a young woman. I looked closer, she looked familiar, who was she? I turned a few more pages and saw a photograph of the same young woman coming down church steps, arm linked through the man's. They had smiling faces, he wore his uniform, she had on a pale suit and a small white hat with a veil just covering her eyes. People were throwing confetti? No, it was more like rice. I carefully took out the photograph and turned it over, in faded ink I could just about read the date 13th May 1944, and the words "the happiest day of my life". I put the photograph back in its place and turned over the page, it was blank and so were the following pages. I wondered what had happened. I put the album back in the drawer and opened one of the cupboard doors, there was an old shoebox inside, I took it out and removed the lid. There were a bundle of letters tied up in a pink ribbon and a newspaper cutting about a bombing raid on Duisburg, Germany on the night of 21-22 May 1944, this raid had destroyed many buildings, but it came at a price, 29 planes were lost. Was this significant I wondered? The rest of the story was on another page, which was missing. Maybe there was more information in the letters, but somehow I couldn't bring myself to read them, they were personal and private.

'What you got there?' John asked.

'Just a pile of old letters' I replied.

'What good are they?' John asked 'I thought you said the old girl was a witch. Ain't no evidence to suggest she is but I found £120.00 under the mattress and half a bottle of brandy so it ain't been a complete waste of time.'

'You can't take her money!' I protested.

'Who's gonna stop me, you? Don't make me laugh!' John said pulling himself up to his full height which was a head above mine.

'C'mon guys let's buy some coke from the all-nighter in the High Street and we'll share the brandy.'

'No thanks' I said, sorry that we had invaded the old lady's home.

'That's good coz you weren't invited anyway' John hissed as he headed for the front door with the other two in tow.

I felt guilty and ashamed. It was all my fault. She'd cured a neighbour's stomach ulcer with a concoction she'd made up from a plant in her garden and I'd listened to all the rumours that followed. Even my sister said to her friends 'That old girl is a real witch. She has a black cat and I'm sure she rides a broomstick at midnight!' She was just a lonely old lady. Then I realized why the girl in the picture looked familiar, it was the old lady when she was younger. I would tell my parents what had happened, all of it. They would be shocked and it might even be that the police would be involved, but I felt it no more than we all deserved. I let myself out the front door, making sure it was closed behind me and headed for home.

HERMIONE WESTON

'Do not be afraid of death'

She could see the young man was shaken. His face pale, eyes wide open.

'It means the death of an old way of life, and a new beginning This second card is the three of Wands. Good foundations have been laid, but hard work is ahead. Are you thinking of leaving your present job and looking for a new one, by any chance?'

'Y-y-yes', he stammered 'I have recently enrolled for a new IT course at college'

'Well then, these are the foundations that have been laid. You are on the right path. It will lead to new opportunities and a new career'

The young man still appeared to be uneasy. He ran his tongue over dry lips and pulled at a loose thread on the high-backed Queen Anne style chair upon which he sat.

'I can see you are still doubtful' she said. 'Shuffle these angel cards and pick one'.

The young man did as he was asked. A card fell to the floor whilst he was shuffling them.

'No, do not put it back in the deck. Hand it to me'.

The young man handed over the card without even glancing at it.

She turned over the card with a well manicured but unvarnished hand, and laid it before him. It had the picture of a cherub with tiny white wings, dressed in a blue toga, it flew next to a stork carrying a baby.

'This confirms what I told you, read it for yourself'

She handed him the card and he read aloud, 'The changes you are experiencing are divinely directed by your newborn willingness to learn new skills and accept the changes that this will bring'

At last the young man smiled and he said 'Thank you. I really enjoyed the reading and your predictions. Although the death card did alarm me at first. How much do I owe you?'

'It's a little over the hour, but we'll just call it forty-five pounds. Is that OK?' Why she asked the question she didn't know because it was the price they had agreed and one she always charged her clients for an hour. Whether it was the Tarot, or an angel card reading, the crystal ball, or sometimes a combination of all three.

'Indeed' the young man said handing over cash. 'And be sure you will see me again soon'.

Before he had a chance to stand up, Hermione's Burmese cat jumped onto his lap and began purring loudly.

'Well if that isn't a good omen, I don't know what is!' she exclaimed. 'It's not everyone Soraya takes a liking to'.

The young man laughed and tickled the cat behind its left ear. Then standing, he placed the cat on a nearby footstool.

'Goodbye' he said, closing the door behind him when he left.

Hermione smiled, Another satisfied customer, she thought, putting the tarot cards into their purple and gold, velvet pouch, the angel cards back into their box.

'Come on Soraya, supper time'

The cat obediently followed Hermione into the kitchen.

* * * * *

Hermione Weston looked out of her ground-floor window and watched her Burmese cat Soraya as she sat in the late evening sunshine washing her whiskers. All appeared to be in order. A warm breeze gently rustled the leaves of the old apple tree and blew in through the open window. lifting the lace curtain as it did so. Soraya, having finished her evening ablutions, arched her back, stretched, then settled down again for a nap in her favourite spot. 'All is well', Hermione said, under her breath, but still, she couldn't shake the feeling of disquiet that had been with her all day. She pondered over the meaning of the three tarot cards she had chosen when making a reading for herself earlier. The first was the Queen of Spears, signifying a woman of deep spiritual strength and understanding. A woman of knowledge, learning, courage, and leadership, who represents independent thought, strength of conviction, with a love of nature. She took this to be herself and had no queries with this card. The second card was The Lovers. She laughed at this. At her time of life, she doubted that a lover was about to enter her life. The second, more likely meaning was the unreserved love of a person or thing. This perplexed her. The only thing she loved in her life without reservation was Soraya, her faithful, unquestioning companion. The third card was Judgement, which usually signifies change, like closing the door on an old job, and opening the door to a new and very different career. But it's also about making a final decision, maybe forgiving an abusive spouse, leaving to make a new life. She could make no sense of them. Best to leave them alone and come back later, or even tomorrow when the meaning would probably become clear to her.

'I will bake an apple and ginger pie' Hermione announced to no-one in particular. 'That will keep my mind occupied', and she set about gathering the ingredients.

Two hours later, as the light began to fade, Hermione lit the oil lamp she had inherited from her father and several candles. She hardly ever flicked on the light bulb, preferring the soft glow and shadows cast by the candles. The smell of baking filled her small kitchen. Hermione looked at the clock, as the sun finally disappeared, it was time to take out the pie and set it to cool. As she bent in front of the oven an eerie feeling swept over her, like an ice-cold hand clutching at her heart. Where was Soraya? She ran to the window, the cat was gone from her resting place. 'Calm down, its dark and she probably came in through the cat flap without you noticing!' Hermione scolded herself. But inside she knew that hadn't happened. The cat flap always made a click-click sound whenever Soraya entered or exited the kitchen. Just the same, Hermione went through the ritual of checking the upstairs sleeping place, under the bed, in cupboards and finally in the shed outside, which was always kept locked. The only thing she found inside was a spider, who scurried away from this intruder into its usually, peaceful world. Hermione locked the shed once more. Where was her precious cat?

A voice drifted through the open window next door. Momentarily distracted, Hermione wondered who Frank Dobbs was talking to. It sounded as if he was talking to his wife, Maisie, but Maisie had died 18 months previously. He pleaded, 'Please forgive me, Maisie, I swear to you it was only one kiss, nothing else happened. You were always the only one for me'. Hermione cleared her throat and said loudly 'Mr Dobbs, do you have Soraya in there with you?' The back door opened and a sheepish looking Frank Dobbs emerged with Soraya in his arms. 'I've told you before, Soraya cannot possibly be the reincarnation of your late wife. She is three years old and humans do not transmigrate to the bodies of animals and vice-versa. Now kindly hand her back to me and we'll have no more of this nonsense!' Frank Dobbs handed the cat back to Hermione and said 'It's the eyes, they're just the same'. He hung his head and retreated through his back door.

'Did the nasty man frighten you?' Hermione enquired as she stroked Soraya's silken fur. The cat jumped from her arms, her golden eyes flashed in the moonlight. Hermione could not be certain, but Soraya appeared to have a smug look on her face, which she knew to be impossible, animals did not express facial emotions. Soraya flicked her tail twice then disappeared into the kitchen through the cat flap.

Half an hour later the phone rang, it was Frank Dobbs.

'Hello, Ms Weston. I am phoning to apologise for my earlier behaviour'

'No harm done', Hermione replied, sitting down on a grey velvet stool next to the telephone table. 'Although I did start to worry when I couldn't find Soraya' At the mention of her name, the cat jumped onto Hermione's knee, playfully patting at the phone wire. Frank Dobbs cleared his throat. 'I wonder if I might ask you for the use of your services, for which I will pay you of course'. 'Do you want a tarot card reading?' Hermione asked, bemused, 'No, I was wondering if you could contact Maisie, on the other side for me' Hermione gasped and Soraya jumped to the floor emitting a low growl before running up the stairs, probably to Hermione's bedroom, where she slept.

'I am not a medium, Mr Dobbs'

'But you are a psychic, aren't you'

'Yes I am, but it's entirely different'

'Explain it to me so I can understand then. I thought it was one and the same'

'A psychic is sensitive to the electrical, magnetic and other energies emanating from an individual's aura or energy field. A psychic is able to access information from the emotional, physical and spiritual parts of the energy field. As the aura contains all the information about a person's life. Tarot, angel cards or crystal balls are just a tool for tapping into this energy field'

'I thought when a person died, their soul or spirit left the body and passed to the other side'

'Yes, that is correct'

'And isn't the soul just a form of energy?'

Hermione paused. Frank Dobbs seemed to know a lot about the other side.

'Much of your information is correct Mr Dobbs, but you are still confusing psychics and mediums'

'I've read lots of books on the subject since Maisie's death. Psychics sometimes receive messages don't they?'

'I belong to a meditation circle. We meet twice a month and yes, I have received messages. Usually, they are answers to a specific personal question I have asked.'

'Maybe if you ask you will receive a message from Maisie'

Curiosity getting the better of her, Hermione ventured 'Do you have a specific question you need an answer to?'

'Yes, oh yes! Then you'll help me?' Hermione felt very sorry for the man, his grief was obviously still acute.

'Do you have anything personal of Maisie's you could bring to me?'

'I have her wedding ring'

'OK. Write the question on a piece of paper and post it, along with the ring, through my letterbox'

'I'll do it right away. How much do you charge?'

'Let's see if I have any results first. We can speak on the matter in a few days'

'I am very grateful....' Frank Dobbs voice broke with emotion and he put the phone down.

Hermione sighed as she looked at a photo of a smiling Maisie in white shorts and a blue tee-shirt, her auburn hair piled high on her head, the sunlight catching the specks in her hazel eyes. The wording on the back read "Maisie, in happier times. Torquay 1999. When Hermione had moved into her own home, Maisie was already very sick, only venturing into the garden on rare occasions. Hermione turned over the platinum ring with grooved edging in her hand. She had allowed herself to be persuaded into something that she was certain would fail. Judgement she thought - the final tarot card. She gave a little laugh, then read Frank Dobbs' note for the second time.

"Maisie, I always loved you from the first day we met at Hampstead Fair. You were the only girl I knew brave enough to ride the Rotor, I was smitten. You were my soul-mate, we did everything together. The night of the office party, Christmas 2003 I made the biggest mistake of my life! It was the night I let my hair down and got drunk, the night I stupidly kissed my boss's secretary. In my defence, I will say that she had been flirting with me all week. When I got home I found that you had been crying, I asked you what the matter was you told me your test results had come back, you had been diagnosed with Stage III ovarian cancer, with extensions to the small bowel.

I didn't even know you hadn't been feeling well. Typical of you to face the tests alone, said you didn't want to worry me unless you had to. You fought bravely for the next two years. I thought you never knew of my indiscretion, until that last night when you asked me if there had ever been anyone else and I said no, I felt the lie stab at my heart. Thirty minutes later you were gone. I think you knew and the guilt has eaten away at my very soul these past years. My question is, have you forgiven me?

All my love, Frank xx"

Hermione was very moved by Frank's tender love note and a single tear ran down her left cheek and splashed onto the paper. 'What a lucky lady you were Maisie Dobbs to have had such a devoted husband' Hermione said aloud. The insensitivity of what she had just said struck her. There was no luck involved when Maisie contracted cancer. Hermione sighed heavily, thinking how cruel life was at times.

Hermione wrapped the items in a purple silk scarf, tying a knot carefully so as not to crease the photo. The bundle she then placed into the drawer of the kitchen table for safekeeping.

'There you are Soraya, in time for supper as usual. I cooked you some minced chicken earlier'. The cat purred and entwined herself around Hermione's legs. 'Get out from under my feet you silly girl. Or how else is mummy to feed you?' She said to the cat, pretending to be vexed but tickling Soraya behind her ears.

Hermione sat in front of her bedroom mirror. She unpinned her hair, placing the hairpins and mother-of-pearl hairslide, into a small wicker basket, closing the lid. Her reflection showed that her steel grey wavy hair still shone from all the lavish attention she gave to it and her skin, though finely wrinkled was as firm as any woman's ten years her junior. She sprayed her pillowcase with lavender essence from an atomizer on her bedside locker, but this night, before climbing into bed she sat on the lilac satin bedspread and spoke out loud, addressing Maisie Dobbs.

'Maisie, if you can hear me I have a message for you from Frank. He says you have always been his one true love and wants to know if you forgive him for his indiscretion back in 2003. If you understand, please give me a sign' Hermione looked from the bedside lamp to the single green candle she had lit before asking the question. The candle flame burned tall and brightly without a flicker. She tried again, this time she decided to be more specific. 'Maisie, if you can hear me please acknowledge by way of the candle' Nothing. 'Maybe she will come to me in a dream' Hermione said, placing the purple scarf underneath her pillow. Hermione blew out the candle, loosened the sheets before getting into bed, turned off the bedside lamp and was fast asleep soon after her head hit the pillow.

That night inevitably, Hermione Dreamt of Maisie.

She was standing in her garden smiling and happy, her long auburn hair shone in the sunlight. She was dressed in bright colours, a red jacket, covering a violet-blue top and yellow trousers. In the next instant, she turned into a parrot and flew up into the branches of an apple tree. Then Frank appeared at his back door, holding a piece of apple in his hand and called out to his wife 'Maisie are you there? Won't you come down and take this peace offering?' He looked towards the tree but the parrot had vanished. He tried again, 'Maisie, I need to know if you have forgiven me'. Hermione could definitely make out a whirring sound and a tiny bird appeared with a yellow speckled head and tail and orange-gold sides. It hovered over Frank's head, wings beating at a fantastic speed. The little creature landed expertly on Frank's outstretched palm and the two disappeared into the house together. – Hermione woke with the dawn light creeping into her room. She took pen and paper from her bedside locker and transcribed the whole dream so she could interpret it later, then went back to bed as she had a full hour before her usual time of rising.

The alarm rang at 6.30. Hermione decided she would shower, and take her morning power walk before tackling breakfast and the dream. She dressed in her purple tracksuit, white socks and trainers, opened a tin of tuna flavoured cat food, scooped it into Soraya's dish with a few cat biscuits sprinkled on top. then set off on the short walk to Highgate Woods. An hour later she sat at the kitchen table, eating porridge with chopped dates, looking at the detailed notes she had made earlier. She went to the bookcase to retrieve her copy of *Birds, divine Messengers* and attempted to interpret the dream.

Hermione and Frank sat in her kitchen drinking coffee, discussing the sudden change in the weather and how warm it was for the time of year, then Hermione told Frank about the dream she had the night before.

'Can you make any sense of it?', Frank asked excitedly.

Hermione chose her words carefully, emphasizing that it was only *her* interpretation of the dream.

'Not at first, I knew of course, that the first bird was a parrot. According to the book, a parrot represents communication'.

'That makes sense', Frank said

'I wasn't certain of the second bird but an internet image search confirmed the little creature to be a hummingbird, which represents forgiveness'

'I knew you could do it' Frank said, his voice choked with emotion. 'Maisie has given me a message through you, she has forgiven me' He stood up and shook Hermione's hand, wiping tears away with the sleeve of his jumper. 'How much do I owe you'

'How about you do a few jobs for me around the garden and we'll call it quits'

'It's a deal. You have made me a very happy man. Maybe I can now move forward with my life. Oh, and I bought this for Soraya' Frank said, pulling a green diamante collar from his pocket.

Hermione was not sure whether Maisie had visited her in that dream or if all the talk about her had manifested itself as a dream. Either way, it had turned out well, she was happy to help Frank.

Having watched a particularly interesting documentary on TV that evening and due to the lateness of the hour, Hermione decided to forego her usual leisurely bath and take a shower before bed instead. The water seemed particularly hot, Hermione had a difficult time adjusting the thermostat and the room soon filled with steam. Ten minutes later Hermione stepped from the shower, put on her bathrobe and couldn't believe her eyes. For the briefest of moments, two words appeared on the bathroom mirror before finally being sucked out by the extractor fan

"Thank you"

TRIKAMPIS

'Have you nothing better to do?'

'No, not really'

'Why don't you go to the library & get a book'

'I'm more of a comic man actually'

'you're sixteen and you still read comics?'

'Yeah, not kids stuff. More like graphic novels'

'Fascinating'

'I think you'd enjoy Twilight or the Vampire Hunter'

'You've got to be kiddin'

'No, it's true. They are very interesting.

'I meant, you've got to be kiddin' if you think I'd read that rubbish'

'Not your kind of thing?'

'No, but don't let me stop you going to the newsagent and buying the latest issue'

'Silly. I buy them from specialist outlets or online at Amazon'

'The library has a computer'

'I have a computer at home'

'Then I suggest you go home and use it'

'I'll walk you to the bus stop'

'I can find my way. I've done it many times, alone!'

'We're catching the same bus. It's better to travel together'

'Better for who?'

'Ha ha. If I didn't know you better, Bryony, I'd think you were trying to get rid of me'

'You catch on fast'

'But it's not safe to walk the streets alone.

It's still light. Nothing ever happens in the daylight'

'That's not true and you know it.'

We'll have to continue this conversation another time, there's my friend Donna'

'How about tomorrow? Same time, same place?'

'No can do. I have an assignment to finish for Science'

How about Tuesday or Wednesday?'

'I'm gonna be busy all week, and next AND the week after that. Bye'

'You can't be busy for ever. It's OK I'm a patient guy. See you tomorrow at school'

'Not if I see you first'

'Always the joker, but it makes me love you even more!'

She ran across the road, narrowly avoiding being hit by a car. She grabbed Donna's arm and without a backward glance, they turned the corner.

He'd said the 'L' word. Bryony was horrified. She had hoped and prayed that she would never hear that word from his lips.

‘What’s up Bry?’ Donna asked.

‘It’s David Marchant. He just said the ‘L’ word’

‘No......really?. How does that make you feel?’

‘He gives me the creeps!’

‘I think he’s kinda cute’ Donna said

‘You are kidding me..... right?’

‘No..... it’s sweet the way he follows you around like a lost puppy’

‘He’s freakin’ me out. He even followed me to the hairdresser last week and was still there when I came out’

‘I think you are over-reacting’ Donna said

‘That’s what Beth said’

‘Well then, she should know. My sister is older and wiser than us’

‘That’s as maybe, but she’s never had a stalker!’

‘Ha ha.....very funny. David is hardly that is he?’

‘It certainly feels like that sometimes.’ Bryony said

‘Didn’t you say that he told you his father died when he was six?’

‘What’s that got to do with anything?’

‘His mother has probably been over-protective to compensate. He’s probably not that experienced with girls’

‘Oh great. Now he’s a mummy’s boy as well as a stalker!’

‘Maybe it’s the blonde hair’ Donna offered

‘Oh my God, what should I do?’

‘I dunno. Seems to me it’s a problem I would grow to like. If it bothers you that much why don’t you dye your hair?’

‘Yeah..... I might just do that’ Bryony replied.

Bryony Lewis looked at the box of mahogany hair dye. ‘Well its certainly different’ she said to herself. But she felt this was the first step in the right direction to get that dummy off her back once and for all. She had drawn the line at cutting short her shoulder length hair – that was just a bit too drastic, besides she hoped the hair dye would do the trick. She applied the dye, making sure she combed it through to the ends of her hair and put on the plastic cap supplied. It was too late to go back now, she sighed and looked at the clock, the leaflet said to leave the colour on for twenty minutes. She wondered briefly if her mother would even notice, so much of her time was spent with this new man in her life. A note was left on the table for Bryony which read ‘dinner in oven, don’t wait up’. Half an hour later, Bryony looked at her reflection in the mirror, well....she certainly looked different. Tears spilled down her cheeks, partly because she had had to take such drastic action and partly because she was left on her own once again. It wasn’t because she couldn’t fend for herself, but she wished her mother was more “normal” like Donna’s mother who was always there for her daughters.

Bryony finished drying her hair then turned off the oven taking out the chicken casserole her mother had made for her, knowing it was her favourite. Bryony scolded herself, 'why shouldn't my mother have a life if she wants one' She felt a bit better as she tucked into her food. She would phone Donna after she had done her homework, she always cheered Bryony up and later she would watch a DVD before going to bed.

The next morning Bryony met Donna at the end of her road, as always. 'You look so different. What did your mum say?' Donna wanted to know. 'She said that she thought it a bit on the dark side but could hardly complain as she was my age when she started to dye her hair' 'Your mum is so cool, I wish mine were more like yours' Bryony didn't tell Donna that she wished her mum were more like hers. Instead, she changed the subject 'Let's get the bus, I feel lazy today, besides I want to hand in my Science Project early' 'And hope to avoid David Marchant at the same time perhaps?' 'Exactly' Bryony laughed as they caught the single decker bus which would drop them outside the school gate.

Her plan had worked, there was no sign of David, but she knew it would only be a brief respite he was sure to be at the school gates this afternoon, waiting for her. 'Catch you later Donna, I still have a few notes to add to this Science Project before handing it in.' 'OK, I'll catch you during break.'

Bryony walked off in the direction of the library. There was no sign of David during the break, and he wasn't waiting for her at the school gate at 3.30, 'Perhaps he is ill' Donna offered. 'Whatever the reason, I'm glad of it. Do you fancy a milkshake on the way home? I'm buying' Bryony said ' I was never one to say no to a free milkshake'

The next day there was no sign of David either, 'It must be my lucky week' Bryony said to Donna. They decided to take a walk through the park as the day was still warm, this shortened their journey by ten minutes. 'I do hope David is OK' Bryony said 'What's this? I thought you couldn't stand the creep – you words not mine' 'Maybe I've been a bit harsh, he's really harmless. If he isn't in school tomorrow I'll call in on the way home to see how he is' Bryony said. The following morning Bryony hung back to see if David was running late, she even waited until the last bell sounded before going into school, but he didn't show'. During break Donna found Bryony with her nose in "Jamaica Inn". 'I have some news for you' Donna said 'Yeah, what's that? 'Seems like David Marchant isn't ill, his friend told me he has been seen with a girl.' 'W-what? I thought he liked me' 'Not jealous are you?' Donna asked 'Don't be daft. Just wondered who the poor girl is. Do you know?' 'No, but it shouldn't be hard to find out.'

All afternoon Bryony couldn't concentrate on any of her lessons, just kept clock watching until the bell rung at 3.30 and it was the end of the school day. As Bryony hung back waiting for Donna, she saw David for the first time in three days. He looked different, his hair was cut in the latest style and he was wearing jeans. He waved when he saw her and Bryony smiled wryly until she realized he hadn't been waving at her. The girl rushed up and kissed him on the cheek, at the same time Donna appeared. 'Must be a relief for you' she said 'I'm curious to find out more' Bryony said ignoring Donna's statement, adding 'Lets follow them and see where they go' David and the girl, who neither of them recognized, seemed oblivious to everyone else, as they headed in the direction of the town centre with Bryony and Donna in close pursuit.

The Coffee House was very busy but that didn't deter Bryony as she went inside. As cooly as she could manage Bryony ordered two cappuccinos 'Four pounds eighty please ladies. Take a seat and I'll bring them over' the assistant said winking. David & his companion sat in a corner booth. Bryony & Donna sat near enough so they could watch but far enough away which could be deemed a respectable distance. The assistant brought the coffees over and winked again. 'Thank you' Donna said gushing. 'No problem' he replied. 'He's cute' Donna said 'Ugh Gross!' Bryony replied. 'You used to say that about David and now we are spying on him' 'We are not spying on him. We just happen to be in the same place at the same time.' 'Oh yeah, right' Bryony sipped her coffee, she didn't like to admit it but she wondered if what Donna had said earlier was true, could she be feeling jealous? She dismissed the thought and looked over just in time to see David and the girl stand up to leave. 'wait 5 minutes and we'll follow them' Bryony said. 'Not me I'm off home and I'm taking you with me so don't even think of protesting' Donna replied.

They caught the little single decker bus which left them at the top of their road. 'I must find out who David's girlfriend is. Yes I Know...I'm becoming obsessed will you help me?' 'Tomorrow is another day. Phone me before bedtime' 'Don't I always?' Bryony said giving Donna a hug.

Bryony was left on her own once again, but this time she was grateful, she would take a long soak in the bath, using some of her favourite Body Shop bath cream, manicure her toes and fingernails and tomorrow she would make an appointment to get her eyelashes tinted. 'I'll show David Marchant just what he's missing.' With her mind made up, she slid into the warm scented water singing along to the song which played on the radio.

The next day was Saturday, usually Bryony would get up late, but not today, she wanted to go for a jog in the park, she put on white shorts and a yellow t-shirt with the words No problem emblazoned in red across the front, white socks and white trainers, she left a note for her mother on the way out and decided that she would make that appointment at the beauticians before coming home again. She closed and locked the door behind her and saw the girl who had been with David the day before. Bryony noticed that although the girl wasn't plain, she could barely be called attractive and wondered why David preferred such a creature to herself. The door to No. 29 opened and David came out and kissed the girl on the cheek in full view of anyone who could be watching. 'Hi David' she called out before she had time to think properly, 'aren't you going to introduce me to your friend?' Of course, Bryony this is Lisa my.....' Bryony put out her hand and shook Lisa's. Nice to meet you' Lisa said 'David has told me all about you' He's told me nothing about you' Bryony said 'Have you known each other long?' 'Yes all of our lives' 'Wud you like to come to a bar-b-que later Bryony? 2 o'clock I can introduce you properly to Lisa' David asked. Bryony thought it a bit odd but asked 'Can I bring Donna?' 'Sure thing'. I'll see you both later.' Bryony decided she would run to the town centre instead of the park, she had already decided what to wear to the bar-b-que, she would have a spray tan as well as her eyelashes tinted at the beauticians, it was all out war now, she meant to re-kindle David's interest this afternoon and the bar-b-que was just the place to do it.

On the way home she called in to see Donna 'You

will come won't you?' 'Of course' 'David said not to bring anything, just ourselves, so I'll call for you at two.' What are you going to wear? Donna asked. My new lemon dress. And you?' 'Shorts & my new t-shirt' 'OK see you later'.

Bryony looked in the mirror, she liked what she saw. The colour in her hair had faded after several washes, and with her hair up she looked more sophisticated. She grabbed a white cardigan on the way downstairs, her mother had left another note, it seemed to Bryony that they communicated only through correspondence lately. She picked up her keys and with one last look in the hall mirror, she was gone.

It was nearer 3 o'clock when Bryony and Donna arrived at the bar-b-que. Bryony had insisted that she didn't want them to be the first ones there. Her eyes scanned the guests and she saw David talking to the girl Lisa. Smiling she walked over to them whilst Donna was getting two glasses of punch. Feint heart never won fair lady, or in this case, boy so she said, 'Hi David, that new Bond film is on in town next week, do you fancy going to see it' 'With you?' 'Yes, with me' 'I would love to'. Bryony looked at David, he did look kind of cute with his new hairstyle. Why hadn't she noticed before? 'Lisa was smiling, she didn't seem at all put out by Bryony asking David for a date. 'By the way, let me introduce you properly. Lisa this is my friend Bryony, and Bryony this is Lisa Marchant, my cousin'.

THE MISSING CHILD

The moon rose over the hill.

In the distance, she could see the lights of the city, bright against the dusk sky. But here on Hampstead Heath, there was only desolation.

It was the middle of winter, very cold. She stood next to a huge oak tree. Its branches would be laden with leaves in Spring and summer offering shelter from the hot sun, but now they were barren and shook in the stinging winter wind.

She pulled up her hood for protection from the harsh elements. Snow began to fall. People scurried about and from this vantage point on the hill, they resembled ants.

Tania Freeman worked in a skyscraper office block at Canary Wharf. She was just a small cog in a huge wheel at the offices of London's fastest selling magazine, ***Votre Sante.*** Her title was Administrative Manager, but anyone with an ounce of common sense could carry out her duties just as efficiently as she. Obviously, the company didn't believe she was capable of anything else at 32, as she had been overlooked twice in the past year for promotion by much younger colleagues.

On an impulse this morning she had decided to phone in sick. She needed the time to be alone, time to decide which direction to take next. Her head was still buzzing with unanswered questions, so she walked on, over the Vale to Parliament Hill.

She sat on an empty bench, feeling lonely and insignificant. Her breath came in clouds of vapour and she wished she were somewhere, anywhere but London, on this very cold January day.

'Hello' a voice broke through her reverie, it took Tania a few moments to gather her thoughts and the voice repeated 'Hello, can you help me?'

Tania looked to her right and saw a small child, about six years old, looking at her with large blue eyes. She had long brown curly hair, kept in place by a pink Alice-band. She wore shiny pink Wellington boots with long grey socks turned over at the top and beige suede mittens with a white cuff. Tania welcomed the interruption, realising that her imposed solitude was not all she hoped it would be.

'Of course, I will help you honey, if I can', Tania said 'What's wrong?'

'I am lost', the child replied.

Tania, realising the seriousness of the situation, looked about her but could see no other adults close by, so she asked the child, 'What is your name sweetheart?' her voice was soothing and gentle, she did not want to distress the child further. 'My name is Amy Liddel, and I am 5 & three quarters' the little girl replied.

'Where is your mummy?'.

'Mummy did not come, we were on the swings'

'Who are we' Tania asked, taking the child's

hand, now worried that she might run off and be abducted.

'My nanny, Aggie, and my brother David' the child said and added 'She was not very happy'

'Why was she not happy' Tania asked, trying to gather as much information as possible.

'David kept asking all day to go to the swings & Aggie said no'

Tania, now spurred into action, walked in the direction of the swings, holding the hand of the small child.

'How did you get separated Amy?' Tania used the child's name, hoping to gain her trust.

'I followed the man with the black puppy' Amy said 'But when I asked him if I could stroke it he was rather cross and said "No - go away little girl". At this point, Amy started to cry, tears streamed down her face, she sobbed, trying to wipe them away with the sleeve of her coffee coloured duffle-coat.

Tania picked up the child to comfort her, at the same time looking around the deserted playground. It was getting darker.

'Excuse me, young lady'. Tania jumped as she felt a hand touch her shoulder. She turned to see a policeman in uniform standing behind her.

'Oh! Am I glad to see you' Tania blurted, before he could say any more.

The policeman's face was expressionless as he

said to Tania 'We have had a report of an abduction and the child in question matches this child's description'.

Tania's mouth fell open as she realised what she was being accused of.

'You think I've abducted Amy?' Tania said, shaking her arm free of his grip, 'I was helping her to find her nanny!'

'It was the nanny, a Miss.... er.... Agnethe Bergstrom who reported the abduction. She said it was a woman with light brown, shoulder-length hair'

'My hair is blonde, not light brown!'

'Well, if you pardon me for saying, it could be mistaken for light brown in the half-light'

'This is ridiculous. I am innocent of the accusation!'

The policeman turned his attention to the child.

'Hello, little girl. Would you like to come to the police station with me?. Miss Agnethe and David are there waiting for you'

Amy's bottom lip quivered. She looked as if she were going to cry again. Instead, she screamed at him, 'No, don't like you.... I want mummy!'

The policeman recoiled as if the child had slapped him.

Amy clung to Tania and wailed 'I want to go home'

Tania bent down in front of the child and offered her a tissue.

'Amy, do you know where you live?'

The child wiped her eyes and blew her nose, handing the tissue back to Tania.

'Yes....I'll whisper' The child leaned closer to Tania and cupped her mouth with her hand.

Tania took pen and paper from her bag, scribbled something and handed it to the policeman.

'Here's Amy's address in Belsize Park'.

'I may have made an error in my judgement' the policeman said begrudgingly to Tania, and to Amy, 'I'm sorry if I frightened you'

Amy said, 'Mummy will be cross with Peter'

'Who's Peter' the policeman and Tania said in unison.

'Peter is Aggie's special friend. She forgets about us when he comes along. They are always kissing. That's why I got bored and went to play with the puppy'

'Hm, I think this warrants further investigation' the policeman said. 'Amy will you come to the station if Miss Tania comes along also?. The vending machine has hot chocolate!' He looked enquiringly at Tania, who nodded her head.

'Oh yes please' Amy said, slipping her small hand into Tania's, as all three headed in the direction of Rosslyn Hill Police Station.

THE BRONZE DRAGON

Jennifer and her friends were bored and the summer holidays were only a third of the way through.

'I'm tired of watching these horror DVDs. Let's do something else' she said

The boys were too busy drinking cider and pretending to be brave through "Halloween", but were not very successful. 'Shit!' Tommy said, spilling half his cider on the coffee table. The other two boys guffawed at Tommy. 'Did you not hear what I said' Jennifer asked adding 'Phwoar, this place smells like a toilet, and Tommy clean up that mess!'

'We'll put The Shining on next' Pete offered.

'I've seen it three times already in the last two weeks. I need some female company, I'm going next door to see if Lucy's in' She could feel Matt's eyes on her. He was very cute but was it worth messing up a perfectly good friendship by getting romantically involved? she wondered as she closed the front door behind her.

She rang Lucy's bell, there was no answer. Jennifer let out a slow, deep sigh. The day was sweltering and humid after the heavy rain that fell all day, the previous day. Jennifer swept her long dark hair up and secured it with a butterfly clip she carried in the pocket of her pale blue jeans. A few moments later the door opened. Lucy stood there in an old tracksuit bottoms and a yellow tee shirt, her pale flaxen hair tied up in a ponytail.

'Hi Jen. I've been grounded by dad after he caught me smoking with Jason. Mum ordered me to clean up my room as in her words "It's like a pig sty"' she said.

'Can you take a break long enough for a quick chat. I

need some feminine company'

'Sure. Do you want a cuppa or something a bit stronger'

'I'd love a coffee'

'Come through to the garden. I'll be out in a minute'

Jennifer headed for the garden table. The umbrella was up affording some shade against the relentless sun. Lucy came out carrying a tray. She had changed into white shorts, which showed off her long, slim, sun-kissed legs, and a white cropped top 'Mum bought a new coffee machine so I've made us two cappuccinos' As she put the tray down, the doorbell rang. 'Damn. Who can that be' she said running back into the house. She came back a few minutes later followed closely by Matt.

'Oh no. Don't tell me, you've set the place on fire!' Jennifer said sarcastically.

'May I sit down?' He asked. 'I've got something to say that might interest you'

Lucy pulled up a third chair 'Sit. This better be good'. Matt sat down close to Jennifer. She looked at Matt as he pushed a brown curly lock of hair out of his eyes. She noticed the subtle smell of cologne he was wearing and the silver chain around his neck with a wolf's head pendant. He turned to Jennifer and smiled, showing even, white teeth. God he was good-looking in a sort of rock star way. Lucy broke the spell. 'Here, you can have my coffee. Spill!' 'OK then. Last week Tommy and I were walking past that empty house, No. 29. It's been up for sale for ages, and we thought we'd take a closer look so we went around the back and found a loose panel in the fence, we loosened it a bit more and managed to get in to the back garden'.

'That's breaking and entering' Lucy said 'You could be in BIG trouble if you were seen'

'Well no-one has come knocking on my door so I think we're safe'

'Alright get on with it' Jennifer said.

'The garden is in a bit of a state. Old, abandoned furniture. A table with a missing leg, upturned broken flower pots. A hosepipe amongst the tall grass and a dilapidated old shed with a locked door'. He paused to take a sip of the coffee. 'Tommy and I had a look around to see if we could find the key and sure enough, there it was beneath an old stone statue of a gargoyle!'

'How weird!' Lucy said.

'It gets even weirder. Inside the shed there were black candles, a pentagram, all different colour crystals, a wand, mirrors, stones with strange symbols, wax & corn dolls, all kinds of figurines including skulls & winged serpents'

'Gross! Those people must have been weirdos!' Jennifer said

'I haven't finished yet, There was also an old tea chest full of books which we tipped up. Beneath a few uninteresting novels was a large book with a purple cover with a gold dragon's crest. Inside were what I can only describe as spells. How to cast a spell to bring wealth into your life. How to bring a lover into your life. How to put a hex on somebody...'

'You're joking right?' Lucy asked

'It's no joke. How to cast runes'

'What are runes?' Jennifer asked, showing more interest.

'They are those stones we found with strange symbols on them'

'Maybe I could cast a spell on Mr Williams, the football coach, to make him fall in love with me' Lucy laughed.

'Are you interested in coming to take a look? I still have the key' Matt questioned with a wry smile.

'Are you kiddin? Course we are!' Jennifer said excitedly.

'OK. To do this properly and if we want to try out some of the spells we have to do this at night!' Matt said.

'Then we should wait til our parents are in bed so we can sneak out. When and where shall we meet?' Lucy asked.

'How about this Friday, it's the 13th. 1a.m. outside the Wishing Well bookshop'

'How appropriate Jennifer said. 'We'll be there'

When Jennifer arrived at the rendezvous point, Lucy was already there. 'I'm not late am I?' she asked.

'No. I couldn't rest. Had a nervous tummy. Don't know if it's fear or excitement'

'Where's Matt?'

'Here' he said and they both jumped as he arrived. 'Do we all have torches?' he asked.

'Yes' the girls replied in unison.

'I thought Tommy might have come?' Lucy enquired.

'He is otherwise engaged with a female!' Matt stated

The three friends set off in silence with Matt in the lead. They reached the fence and Matt pulled back the loose slat letting the girls through first. 'Torches on but pointing downwards' he whispered. The girls did as they were told. A commotion greeted them at the end of the garden as two cats fled and jumped over the fence into next door's garden, spooked by the intruders.

'Shit!' Jennifer said, taking a step back.

'Not so loud. We don't want to wake neighbours! Matt scolded

'OK. I get it. But that commotion scared the hell out of me!' Jennifer responded.

Over to the right and leaning heavily on an already broken fence, stood the remains of the shed.

'No wonder this place hasn't been sold. Too much work needs to be done' Lucy said.

'Yeah and there's probably a nest of rats somewhere. Those cats were more than likely looking for their supper!' Jennifer exclaimed in hushed tones.

Matt took the key from his pocket and put the key in the lock, it grunted and then the door fell open. Matt grabbed it before it had a chance to thud against the fence. 'Ladies first' he said.

Jennifer entered, followed by Lucy then waited for Matt as he pulled the door closed and looped the piece of cord tied to the door over a hook. 'OK girls, there are a few old cushions in the left-hand corner if you want to make yourselves comfortable' he said.

Jennifer shone her torch around the shed, resting her gaze for a moment on each of the figurines.

'Look what I've found' Lucy said, showing them both a Ouija board.

The girls continued to look around the shed, whilst

Matt upturned the tea chest and sat on it with the book in his lap.

Jennifer was fascinated by a dragon figurine. It was bronze in colour and sat upon a crystal ball. It's green glass eyes stared back at her and its mouth was open showing sharp teeth and a red tongue. 'What've you got there Jen?' Lucy asked.

'It's a dragon. I'm kinda drawn to it'

'Put it back and sit down' Matt said. But Jennifer wrapped the dragon in a piece of cloth & stuffed it into the pocket of her Gillet.

'How do you cast a spell to make somebody fall in love with you?' Lucy asked.

Matt found the appropriate page. 'Ok. Shall I read it out?'

'Oh yes please. This is fun' Lucy said

'First you need a red candle, to signify love'

'Here's one' Jennifer said

'Next a piece of white paper and a red crayon'

'My brother has a set of coloured crayons' Lucy said

'You also need a photograph or a lock of hair from your intended victim' Matt laughed

'Go on. What else?'

'Write down everything you wish him to be. Kind, sexy, chivalrous, a good listener perhaps? We always get accused of not listening to girls!'

'Ha ha. Very funny'

'Then on a night when there will be a full moon, you gather the objects together on your prepared altar'

'I don't have an altar' Lucy said.

'Just clear a space somewhere private, where you won't be disturbed. You also need an old coffee tin'

'My mum has plenty of those!'

'Light the red candle. Drip some wax from the candle onto the written list and photograph and by the light of the full moon say these words. "Mother moon I ask tonight, If you will help me in my plight. My love for.....insert name....is pure and true, this is what I promise you. Let him look upon no other. I will take him as my lover, then our hearts will beat as one our journey together has begun". Then you set the picture and the list alight with the flame of the candle and put them into the coffee tin where they will extinguish. You must then bury the ashes in the ground outside your front door to invite him into your home. And if that doesn't work you can always put a hex on him!' The three friends laughed.

'How about some hot coffee?' Jennifer asked.

'Wow that would be great! If only we had some' Lucy said

'Then it's just as well I brought a flask of it in my duffle bag, isn't it?'

'Why do girls always think of practical stuff?' Matt questioned

'Because boys are too busy trying to impress us!' Jennifer teased

When they'd finished coffee Lucy asked 'How about we give the Ouija board a try?'

'I've always heard you shouldn't mess around with things you know nothing about' Jennifer remarked

'There's instructions here so where's the harm?' Matt

asked 'Besides there's three of us here together and if anything odd should happen we'll stop straight away'

'OK' Jennifer agreed reluctantly

There was a round stool beneath some sacking so they placed the Ouija board on top and sat around it.

'First we must hold hands and ask Archangel Michael for protection' Jennifer said

'I hope he's not busy elsewhere or he might be annoyed if we call on him!' Mat quipped

'Don't joke. This is serious' Jennifer scolded

'OK, OK, sorry what should we say?'

'Archangel Michael may your light surround us;

May your love enfold us;

May your power protects us;

We ask that you watch over us;

Now and forever, amen.' Jennifer recited

'Amen' said the other two in unison

They lit two candles. A white one for purity of spirit and a gold one for protection.

They placed an upturned glass upon the stool then held hands again

'Is there anybody there?' Lucy asked

Silence, except for the wind that seemed to spring up out of nowhere. It shook the door and blew over some flower pots in the garden.

'If there's anyone there, please give us a sign' Matt said

The white candle flickered and the glass began to move and spell out the word "Yes"

Lucy gasped and Jennifer said 'Shush'

'Will you tell us who you are?' Matt asked

The glass began to move again. P-R-A-Y-F-O-R-M-E

'Pray for me' Lucy said 'Who are you?'

The glass moved again L-O-S-T

'Lost, we can't help you unless you tell us who you are!' Matt said

The glass moved again. T-H-I-E-F! T-H-I-E-F! T-H-E-I-F! it spelt and the white candle blew out, a branch smashed against the window and a bolt of lightning hit the chimney pot on the roof of the house, sending a shower of stone crashing to the ground..

'Shit!' Lucy yelled 'Let's get out of here quick'

The three friends leapt to their feet and scrambled through the broken fence, forgetting to lock the shed door behind them. They ran as fast as they could until they reached Lucy's house. They sat on the front lawn gasping for breath. 'What just happened?' Lucy asked

'I sure as hell don't know, but I don't mind admitting it scared the crap out of me!' Matt spluttered.

A light came on in Lucy's bathroom window 'Time for me to sneak back into the house before I'm missed.' She said

'Not a word of this to anyone, right?' Matt said 'C'mon Jen, I'll walk you to your door'

They reached Jennifer's door. 'Thanks Matt' she said kissing him on the cheek. 'What for?' he asked. 'Just for being there' 'Any time' he said and walked off.

That night Jennifer had a strange dream. She dreamt that she was back in the garden but as an onlooker. The garden was tidy and the scent of roses wafted her way.

Two children, a boy and a girl played happily with a yapping brown puppy. The boy threw a ball, the puppy chased it but ran past into the bushes. The girl gave chase and emerged shortly after crying & sobbing.

'What's the matter?' the boy asked trying to comfort the girl.

'It's gone' she wailed 'Someone has stolen it'

'Let's look together' he said 'Maybe it's just hidden somewhere' He gave the girl his handkerchief, took her by the hand and walked towards the bushes with the little puppy in pursuit.

'Wouldn't you like to see them happy again' a voice asked in Jennifer's head.

'Of course I would' she answered.

'Then you must return it to its rightful owner' The voice said.

Jennifer woke with a start. She looked over towards her window ledge and saw the dragon's green eyes shining in the moonlight. The mouth with its red tongue seemed to be mocking her. She knew what she had to do first thing in the morning. Once decided she turned over and drifted off into a dreamless sleep.

Sandra Turner

Available worldwide from

Amazon

---

www.mtp.agency

www.facebook.com/mtp.agency

@mtp_agency

Printed in Great Britain
by Amazon

81239545R10068